FREE
LEGAL ADVICE

INDIANA

J. GREGORY GARRISON

Guild Press
Emmis Publishing, LP

GUILD PRESS EMMIS PUBLISHING, LP
10665 Andrade Drive
Zionsville, Indiana 46077

The Guild Press website is
www.guildpress.com

ISBN 1-57860-111-8
Library of Congress Catalogue Card Number 2002107943

Cover Design by Lloyd Brooks, Thrive, Inc.
Interior and Text Design by April Altman Reynolds

Printed and bound in the United States of America

NOTICE AND DISCLAIMER

This book is offered for the purpose of providing a general overview of the law and its applications in Indiana. Nothing contained herein should be construed as specific legal advice, and the opinions and statements contained herein should *in no event* be relied upon for any purpose without the independent and specific advice of competent legal counsel, retained for the specific purpose of providing that assistance. The sole purpose for which this book is offered is to give the reader a general overview of the laws of the State of Indiana and to assist the reader in coming to such understanding. It is not proffered for the purpose of forming the basis for important business or personal legal decisions, and the reader must understand that independent personal legal counsel is imperative in making important decisions. The author, publisher, agents, parent, related and subsidiary entities of either or both hereby disclaim any and all liability for losses or damages of whatever kind or nature that might arise from the opinions, recitations, or accounts contained herein.

CONTENTS

FOREWORD

The first time I signed my name to a pleading and filed it in court, my hand shook so badly that my already-poor penmanship collapsed altogether. There was something metaphysical about the concept of actually representing the interests of another person in court that left me weak in the knees. Over the following twenty-eight years I have been privileged to do so thousands of times, from matters as complex and high profiled as the prosecution of Michael Tyson and the federal litigation involving Steak 'n Shake and Pepsi Cola to hundreds of divorces, small claims actions and personal injury and business disputes where the litigants were local folk with no claim to fame or notoriety. I have tried hundreds—if not thousands—of cases, in most of the county seats of Indiana, as both plaintiff and defendant, driven at least a hundred thousand miles around the state doing so, in the process making a living as a pretty ordinary lawyer. And there could have been no greater calling for me than to do so.

It has been this lifetime of being a lawyer to ordinary people, involved in ordinary struggles and facing, at times, extraordinary problems, that has shaped and molded my views on the art and alchemy of "lawyerin'" Hoosier style, and the honor has been all mine. I have often said that the old cases bear no value beyond lessons learned, as one can seldom find a case that invokes fond memories after it is finished. And the reason for all that is clear, although folks have a hard time with it: The law is involved with the resolution—or at least the adjudication of—broken relationships, misunderstandings, failed dreams and expectations, and even the blackest of express malice. Those who would require or even expect perfect results do not understand the vagaries, the prejudices, the passions and the twisted fate that attends life in modern America. And it is because I have come to recognize just how fine an institution and also what a colossal disappointment the law is to many, that I have decided to provide this book of free advice.

ACKNOWLEDGMENTS

There is no such thing as an easy book. Even one that is modest in size and scope, like this one, requires time, attention, and lots of support. As is always the case, I have had huge help in the preparation of this volume, and that list must start with the good folk at *Indianapolis Monthly*, specifically Debbie Paul, whose brainstorm got the whole thing started, and Nancy Baxter at Guild Press for her consummate good will and steadfast faith that the job could get successfully done.

To my law partners, Mike Kiefer and brother Chris, my hat's off for proofing and reviewing text for its accuracy on the various subjects we have addressed here. These guys are good, and having their input and support has been ever so valuable. The same applies to one of the guys who broke me into this crazy business way back in 1973, Jim Sandifer. He reviewed the chapters on probate and death tax matters, and as has been true for almost thirty years together, his advice was right on the money.

But most of all, it was once again my wife, the notorious Phyllis Jean, who really kept me going. She contributed significantly to the text, corrected and reviewed the whole thing, and provided the encouragement necessary to get me out of bed early each morning to fire up the computer and get this thing written. As always, she is my light.

INTRODUCTION

Let me begin with these few precepts, some lessons learned the hard way over many years. Most are just common sense, but then experience tells us that is a commodity all too scarce these days. If you find yourself in some kind of dispute, negotiation or trouble, here is my advice to you:

1. Get counsel. It costs far less than you would imagine, and the state is full of competent people who know far more than you will ever fathom about whatever your problem may be. The old adage that says "he who represents himself has a fool for a client" is as true as any line in Holy Writ, and going naked first then seeking help later can often spell disaster, even where the case might have been strong in the beginning.

2. Grow up. If you've been arrested, sued, summoned, cited, or subpoenaed, it's all just a part of living in a civilized and just society. Whether it's jury duty or a felony arrest warrant, there are rules that govern the whole affair, and storming around, panicking, hiding out, or otherwise acting silly, will accomplish nothing. In the emergency room of the hospital the doctors have a rule: when a patient codes, the first thing you do is to take your own pulse.

3. Keep records. We live in a complex society, one that at times requires us to prove what we claim to be true. Leases, tax returns, check registers, insurance policies, old wills, title policies, motor vehicle records, and even old college and high school transcripts can be important. Ten years is a good rule of thumb, and taking the time to keep records in a way that lets you find things is not evidence of a sick mind. It can be the difference between winning and losing in a matter that might amount to real money—or even your continued freedom.

4. Tell the truth—*all the time*. Beyond the moral implications of this edict, lying is really stupid. Nothing, and I do mean *nothing*, destroys one's credibility and reputation faster than being untruthful. And in the information age, it can be really difficult to hide a dishonest statement. Besides, your mother taught you better.

5. Respect authority. Courts, judges, cops, even the IRS, are the law. What they say *is* the law for the moment, and violating court orders, arguing with the police, hiding records, or otherwise messing with what might be evidence in a proceeding that concerns you, can only hurt. Remember that all these people put their pants on one leg at a time, just like you do, and while they may be the law at the moment, our wonderful system of justice provides the right to challenge what they say and do, at the appropriate time and in the appropriate way.

6. Read before you sign. Of course you have no chance of really negotiating the language of a lease, an automobile purchase agreement, a credit card contract or zoning ordinance, but if you read it before you sign it, you will have the luxury of having some clue as to what you have agreed to do. No one ever looked more stupid in court than when he admitted he had executed a document obligating him to do or pay something without reading it first.

7. Nothing is free. When you consider offers that appear to be too good to be true, you are correct. They are too good to be true. In this age of glitz, fast talk, hype and gusto, much of what we hear, see and read is untrustworthy. Greed is a really silly sin, capable of producing the most ridiculous cases of temporary insanity, blindness and stupidity.

8. The last guy to get mad wins. Whether it's a marriage, a partnership, a traffic citation or an NFL contract, temper and discourteous behavior almost always define the loser. Righteous indignation is very different from a tantrum, as the former can paralyze the opposition while the latter typically accompanies failure. Whether it's the judge, opposing counsel, your ex-spouse or the cop who arrested you, showing your backside is categorically never calculated to help you win.

9. There are no perfect cases. Compromise is an ugly word to everyone who really believes in his or her cause, or case. But it is not a perfect world, and the sooner you recognize and embrace the reality that compromise is guaranteed, the sooner you will stop spending money on lawyers and be able to go on with your life. It's a mighty thin sheet of paper that has only one side.

    10. Keep your mouth shut. Neither your neighbors, your buddies, the new love of your life, nor the news media—*especially the news media*—will decide your case. So don't tell them about it. There is no "court of public opinion" for most of us, so unless you think you are O. J. Simpson, don't talk.

CHAPTER ONE
⚖ Personal Injury

MOST OF THE JURY TRIALS IN WHICH I HAVE PARTICIPATED AS A CIVIL LAWyer have been as a plaintiff's attorney. And clearly they are all a trip to the roulette wheel for both sides. One of my favorite lawyers, Richie Hailley, once told me "if you want me to get you a million dollar verdict, just bring me a three million dollar case." Wise counsel for sure, and the fact is that juries are pretty unpredictable, as any trial lawyer will tell you. Let's look at the various kinds of claims that courts recognize, and we'll provide a road map for you to follow if you find yourself on one side or the other of such a case.

AUTOMOBILE ACCIDENT CASES—*PLAINTIFF*

If you are hurt in a motor vehicle accident, depending on how badly you have been injured, you may not focus on the details necessary to make sure you can get a fair recovery for yourself or someone in your family. As I said in my introduction, you simply must keep good records. This means more than just making sure you get the other driver's personal and insurance information. It means keeping receipts for rented crutches, over-the-counter and prescription medications, correspondence from your own insurance carrier, and the like. Here is a starter list of the things you should keep in mind:

1. Police or other agency traffic accident reports. If you can do it at the scene of the accident, get the important stuff right there, including the personal and insurance information about the other driver, his or her plate and driver's license number, place of employment, and the name and badge number and police agency of the officer

making the report. You would be surprised how many people can't remember whether the officer's uniform was brown or blue! If this can't happen for some reason, get to work on it (or have someone do it for you) at once, even if you must do so from a hospital bed. *Reason: not everyone tells the truth at these times, and having the details will guard against losing track of the other guy before getting a claim in place. Also, not every detail the officer notes necessarily makes it into the report, and talking to him may be the only effective way of finding some jerk who has done a disappearing act after the accident.*

2. Start a file for medical expenses and other information at once. My partner's paralegal will tell you this file can take months to reconstruct if the client has not done it, and what you collect is likely to be more complete than what we try to put together later. It is probably the best thing you can do to help us eventually evaluate your claims for injuries and associated losses. Remember these things:

a. Keep all receipts for medications—whether or not prescriptions are required for them. Keep receipts for bandages, dressings, braces, wheelchair rentals, and even crutches, whether or not prescriptions are required for them.

b. Keep the little slip they give you at the doctor's office when you check out each time—this will include the uninsured "co-pay" that you may have to pay at the time service is rendered by the physician. The same kind of slip of paper should be saved if they give one to you at physical therapy.

c. Keep the "explanation of benefits" documents that come from your health carrier. They call these "EOBs," and they are very helpful in keeping track of what the injuries are costing, whether or not you are paying or the company is doing so for you. Keep in mind here that there is a fair chance you will end up in an argument with the health carrier before it's over. Just like every other insurance company in the world, they seek to cut costs, and some can be expected to deny coverage, cut payments, or procrastinate for months in making reimbursement to your healthcare providers. *See the chapter on health law for other important aspects of this problem.*

d. Make sure you keep a good list of all the healthcare professionals you see in any capacity, beginning with your family physician or the emergency room person. The ER doctor will be identified on the chart created when you are seen there. This should include the chiropractor, the dentist you consult if you have injury to your mouth or teeth, the eye doctor or the folks at the immediate care facility if you have occasion to visit them for some kind of treatment related to the accident.

3. If the accident drew public interest sufficient to produce news coverage, keep the newspaper clippings and maybe even videotape television coverage. If you can't get this done, remember that the footage from that story will be available from the station carrying it, and getting a copy is typically not difficult. More than once we have been able to resolve conflicting claims about the situation at an accident scene by reviewing news footage of the whole thing. Your lawyer should know how to contact and deal with television stations to get this done, and as I said, they tend to be cooperative, so long as they get their stuff back and you agree to pay for the cost of copying the tape.

4. Keep every scrap of paper, no matter how trivial, that comes from either your own auto insurance company or the other guy's carrier. Sad to say, the era of trusting even your own carrier is gone. And when the same company covers both you and the other driver, things can get really messy. There are just no "good hands" anymore.

5. If you have conversations with either carrier or get lucky enough to talk to the other driver, make an immediate note of what was said in the conversation. This is what the rules of evidence call a "contemporaneous memorandum" and can be almost as good as live testimony in a trial. The same holds true for what folks say at the accident scene. If you can do it, write down what was said as soon as possible after leaving the scene, date it, and keep it with these records. At least a hundred times, I have seen cases where the other guy falls all over himself at the scene, apologizing profusely, offering assistance, and making clear admissions of liability. However, once his own carrier has gotten to him, or he has had a chance to cool off, those statements disappear, and he will deny ever having spoken to you *at all!* In one case we tried recently, a woman failed to see a red light and plowed into the back of our client's car when he was stopped at an intersection. He was hurt but most of the injuries didn't start showing up until a few hours later, so he got out of his car and talked with her. She was ever so sorry, cried, and was most solicitous for his well-being. Not so at trial, however, or even in her deposition. I guess the realities changed after the lawyer had a visit with her. So write it down at once.

6. The repair estimates, tow records, actual costs of repair, car rental, taxi fares necessitated by being without a car, actual repair bills and receipts, and copies of insurance checks paying for that damage are all important. Too often companies get difficult over fixing your car or try to get in your pocket when valuing the vehicle if it is, in their opinion, a total loss. It's a dirty trick, but they can push an insured around pretty effectively if they combine an unfair offer for the damaged vehicle with a decision to terminate rental car coverage. "This is how much we will pay for your old jalopy. Oh—and by the way—turn in your rental car in the morning." "But that's an unfair value for my fine, low-mileage ride, and you know it. And besides, how will I get to work or to the doctor if you stop my rental

car coverage?!" Just the point. They've gotcha. The rental car is history, so you must take the insufficient offer on your own car so you can use it to go buy another. We can help there, but only if we have these records that tell us what happened to the car and how much it's really worth. In one case, the air bags failed to deploy upon impact, and we were interested in examining the wreck for evidence of failure. The company was in the process of moving and destroying the vehicle when we tracked it down and prevailed on them to hold it until we could determine whether or not the air bag issue was real.

Note: Your own photos of your damaged car may be very useful at trial. Before the car is repaired or declared "totaled" and sold for parts or crushed, you or a friend should take pictures, inside and out. Do not count on the insurance company to do this. A really important feature here is the detail included in the pictures. Photos taken at the wrecker yard in poor light or after a fresh snow has fallen are of little use. Damage location and severity, multiple impact points, condition of tires and even brake pads can be crucial, and I can say from looking at thousands of photos, such detail is seldom present in the instant-develop type photos those guys take.

7. Finally, keep copies of all correspondence you receive from the police or the Bureau of Motor Vehicles. If there is confusion over "financial responsibility" on either side, that is, the existence and extent of insurance coverage, BMV will be corresponding with the parties. Also, in cases where liability for the accident—fault—is an issue, official actions taken by the police to charge one side or the other with traffic violations in connection with the accident are crucial. It's difficult to maintain that one is not at fault when the cops have charged you with reckless driving. So keep this stuff that comes to you, and if the other side is charged with violations, follow up with the authorities to make sure you know what happens. Staying in touch with the prosecutor may be the best way to accomplish

this, so the case doesn't slip through the cracks and disappear. You really want that conviction for reckless driving, speeding, disobeying signals, or drunk driving against the other guy to happen. Several times I have been retained to assist accident or other crime victims as a liaison with the police and prosecutor's offices, keeping track of the progress and disposition of cases like these. Your accident lawyer should do so, because having serious criminal charges slip through the cracks of the court system can really hurt your position when settlement—or trial—time comes along. Most prosecutors can be counted on not to deal away drunk-driving cases where an accident with injuries has been part of the equation. However, as the bumper sticker says, "Stuff Happens," and incompetence, administrative error, missed court dates, and even the rare but possible instance of collusion between authorities and the defendant do occur. Remember that victims are entitled to notice with regard to all portions of any criminal proceeding that deals with pleas and sentences. And you can imagine how much more attentive the judge will be— and how much harder it will be for a deputy prosecutor to mess things up—if your shining face is there every time.

It may seem like a lot of trouble, but I can tell you from experience that nothing is more helpful to the lawyer's staff in commencing work on a new case than having a client who has kept some good records. You can't keep too much, but it's very easy to keep too little.

▶ *The Law*

People are entitled to recover for injuries and other damages suffered in an accident if those injuries and damages are caused by that accident and the accident is the fault of the other driver. So your lost wages, pain and suffering, damaged clothing, lost vacation, damaged car, permanent impairment caused by the injuries, and even lost "consortium" for your spouse—the idea of lost services caused by injuries—are compensable in Indiana. We are, however, a "comparative fault" state, so that, in an accident where both parties have been negligent, a jury can find that any award of damages must be reduced according to that percentage of fault attributable to the plaintiff. Most of this will be covered by your lawyer, who will take all those factors into account in valuing your case for settlement purposes. So in an intersection accident where one party was driving too fast and the other failed to obey a traffic signal or sign, comparative fault will be an issue.

Some driver error or misconduct is so obvious and so dangerous that no one really argues about liability in those cases. If the defendant was drunk or under the influence of drugs, or if he was operating a vehicle that was clearly unsafe, liability discussions are typically pretty short. And where reckless behavior is present, again including driving drunk or stoned, engaging in drag racing, or running a stoplight at high speed during rush hour, there is the possibility of a jury awarding punitive damages.

Lawsuits claiming damages for personal injuries or property damage must be filed within two years of the date the claims arose. That typically means the date of the accident. So nobody should mess around after being hurt. As you can see from the previous checklist, there are many things to be considered and much to be done before a plaintiff can effectively prosecute a case; getting counsel early is very important. Moreover, witnesses move away, change jobs, die, or go to jail, while police officers get transferred or lose their records or forget what they saw or did. Doctors retire or move to other offices, and records get lost. There is more to this sense of urgency than just the two-year statute of limitations. One thing to remember, however, is that when minors are involved as plaintiffs their claims are not cut off by the two-year statute of limitations until two years *after* they reach eighteen years of age. So even if the child is injured when he or she is very young, they still have until two years after their eighteenth birthday to file suit. This also makes sense because kids have many problems with injuries that do not affect adults. Fractures to bones that involve growth plates, scars that will cause more disfigurement as the tissues around them grow, or damage to organs, skeleton, or muscles that will inhibit development are all problems that adults don't face.

One such case we handled for a father and son included severe leg injuries to a thirteen-year-old boy whose fractures were in what the doctors call "growth plates." Unless that very important segment of the long bone heals well enough for that plate to continue functioning, the leg will not grow at the same rate as the other, causing a myriad of problems that will probably have life-long consequences.

Folks who are not competent to care for or make decisions for themselves may require a guardianship, so there can be some court-appointed person who is obligated to protect their interests. Again, this is lawyers' work, and whomever you choose to represent that person, the lawyer will be responsible for recognizing those problems and dealing with them as the law requires.

▶The Facts

As we all know, there are no perfect cases. In every case, there are disputes over who, what, how, when, where, and how much, and those who work in this area recognize that those problems will always be there. Evaluating factual issues is what lawyers are trained to do, so most of your concerns over such facets of the case will have to include them. In short, be prepared for arguments and counter-arguments, but don't let them worry you. They play an important role in the evaluation process, but they are not the only part. How badly you are hurt, the nature of the injuries suffered, and the way the law addresses the issues in the case are also important. Facts are the foundation, but not the whole ball game.

▶The Lawyer

It has become the age of specialization in this area, and the onslaught of advertising has really served to tell the public that only certain firms are the right choice. Well, certainly there are several very good lawyers who so limit their practices and invite the public to employ them. And it is also true that the lawyer who wrote your will, handled your divorce, or represented your brother-in-law in his drunk-driving case, is not necessarily the right choice for your personal injury lawyer. However, that also does not rule that attorney out. I still have great respect for the general practice bar in Indiana, and it is still true that those with a broader knowledge and experience in the practice—and especially in the courts—can bring important skills to your case. With all that said, here are some criteria to consider:

1. Experience is critical. If a firm has not handled several personal injury cases in the past, it is most likely a bad choice. Just like every other walk of life, the personal injury practice has its own vocabulary, its own customs and practices, and *its own rules*. So ask the right questions. How many cases has it handled, and of what variety? What percentage of its practice is devoted to injury cases? The answers will tell you quickly whether or not it passes the experience test.

2. In-house and outside resources make the case. The firm should have ready access to health care professionals who assist in collecting, organizing, and evaluating medical information. Some of the lawyers best known in the area will have a nurse or other professional on staff; others maintain a contract relationship with such folks, so they can efficiently make sense out of hundreds of pages of medical records. They should have ready access to a good investigator, an accident reconstruction expert, and other specialists who can address technical issues like brake failures, engine problems, air bags, automatic signal malfunctions, and a whole array of other factors that may play a role. We once had to hire a witness to testify about whether or not a defendant had operated a speed boat safely, another to address how a hazardous substance was handled, and even one to talk about how the injury affected the guy's tennis game.

3. What's the courtroom experience factor? There should be lawyers in the place who can do more than take depositions and read hospital charts. You still need to be represented by lawyers who know their way around a courtroom, because even though the vast majority of cases are settled,

the insurance companies know who can try cases and who cannot. If they don't respect your lawyer as a courtroom advocate, they will be much more likely to roll the dice with a jury than if they know the guy is likely to knock their heads off in trial.

4. Attorneys' fees. It's a contingent fee world today, and the old traditional 1/3 fee is still pretty much the rule, although it is now common for the arrangement to bump to 40% if suit or trial is required and even 50% in the event of an appeal. Trials are rare, and appeals are even more so, but those provisions are common in contingent fee contracts. **All contingent fee agreements are required by law to be in writing.** If that doesn't happen, you have a pretty good indication that the lawyer doesn't do much of this kind of work. You will have to agree to pay your own expenses, either as they are incurred or at the end, out of the amount you recover. You should understand that the expenses are not fees, and the firm will expect you to pay them, win or lose. Not so with the fees. If they lose, they make nothing.

▶ Evaluating Damages
"Nobody Knows the Trouble I've Seen"

The most difficult part of preparing a case for settlement negotiations, whether or not through mediation, is coming to some consensus between the lawyer, the physicians, and the injured party on the subject of valuation. To the person with chronic pain and a real loss of life function, whether related to work or to leisure pastime, it's easy to feel like nobody is listening. What may seem like career-ending injuries or devastating losses to plaintiff and family may or may not amount to damages for which a jury will award money.

The biggest and most difficult of all these is what the medical/legal world calls "soft tissue injuries," the old "whiplash" syndrome. Reflexive Sympathetic Dystrophy Syndrome (RSDS), Chronic Fatigue Syndrome, various sciatic nerve and other neurological phenomena, and just good old low back pain all can ruin a person's life. Over the years we have seen and represented folks with all these, and all can be really difficult to diagnose, assess, and prove. The problem here is the subjective nature of the claims, and that comes from the absence of objective findings in the medical workup. Chronic pain and loss of function to the patient characterize all those previously mentioned problems. However, none of them are typically accompanied by objective proof, like a bad disc in the spine, a broken bone, a torn rotator cuff, ligament or cartilage tear, severed nerve, identifiable muscle damage, or even a good nasty bruise. Folks whose daily struggles with pain make them acutely aware of how badly they are hurt have real trouble facing the concept that their injuries have finite dollar value to a jury or a court. Low speed impacts sometimes cause severely painful injuries. One client suffered terrible damage to her spinal column in a case where the impact was at less than ten miles per hour. However, the defendant was driving a 30,000-pound semitrailer rig, and the energy imparted to her little car was huge. Nevertheless the major detractor to her case valuation was the absence of any physical finding that seemed consistent with such a low speed hit. The case finally settled, but the numbers were far less than the injuries might have been expected to bring had the facts been different.

It makes no sense to go through a long list of possibilities here, but the short answer is that you need people representing you and caring for you medically who are skilled at these kinds of evaluations. Today there are specialists in medicine who spend their whole practices doing nothing but assisting folks who deal with chronic pain, permanent injuries, and even the psychological damage that often accompanies being hurt. Occupational Medicine is of huge assistance here, as is that branch of neurology that deals with pain management. Orthopedic specialists are able to evaluate the amount of impairment a body suffers from an injury and to reduce it to a percentage explanation that the world will understand. Here is a partial list of those losses that may be compensated:

1. Lost income—past, present, and future

2. Property damage

3. Loss of services from a spouse (this includes companionship, sexual relationship as well as just plain affection, and that spouse's ability to manage their part of the family workload)

4. Pain and suffering for bodily injury

5. Emotional upset

6. Loss of support from a spouse or parent (see also Wrongful Death)

7. Permanent loss of function

8. Disfigurement

I finish as I began here, urging anyone who has been injured in an accident to seek competent counsel early in the whole recuperation process. Again, the only good hands you can count on are those of your physician and your lawyer.

AUTOMOBILE ACCIDENT CASES—*DEFENDANT*

There is only one rule here: buy good insurance and tell the company at once when you have been in an accident. If at fault, your company owes you the affirmative duty of representing your interest, shielding you from personal liability exposure, paying for property damage you may have caused, and dealing with those who claim injuries. This includes all phases of the case, from initial information gathering to ultimate disposition of all claims, either through trial or settlement. The claims adjuster or evaluator assigned to your case by your insurance company will be responsible for collecting, reviewing, evaluating, and countering all information regarding the accident.

Your job is to cooperate with the company in all reasonable ways, providing statements, documents, pictures, and reports, as well as answering questions and assisting them in obtaining information that you may have access to. Again I say, keep your mouth shut. Avoid volunteered statements, and do not give a statement to anyone over the phone or in person unless your company knows about it first and consents to it. This will probably happen, but your continued coverage depends on your cooperation, and this includes not making things worse by talking when you should not. Of course, this does not include law enforcement personnel. If the case includes claims or charges against you of a criminal nature, GET COUNSEL Do not talk to anyone about the case unless your defense lawyer says it's okay to do so. This can, in some cases, include your insurance adjuster. In a case where claims are made against you for drunk driving, reckless driving, speed contests, and the like, you have no friends except the lawyer who represents you, and the insurance company will not provide such a person. At the moment you determine that you might be charged with a traffic offense such as those listed above, talk to no one and hire a good criminal defense lawyer at once. We'll further address that decision in our chapter on criminal law.

In a civil case, counsel chosen by the company will represent you, and those lawyers are routinely very good at what they do. Even though their fees are paid by your carrier, they represent your interest. In a case where the damages are claimed to be greater than the extent of your coverage, it is, however, a good idea to have counsel independent of the company. You have to pay those fees yourself, but, if you have assets in your own name that might be exposed to the claims of a plaintiff whose injuries are claimed to be bigger than the limits on your policy, some early planning and coordination with the lawyer provided by the company is a very good idea. I represented a business whose car had caused huge damages to a plaintiff, and even though the insurance policy provided over a million dollars in coverage, the defendant company had us negotiate on its behalf to minimize the contribution they would have to make toward settling the case. Of course, the best defense against this awful eventuality is to make sure you have adequate coverage. The state requires only a minimum of $25,000 in liability coverage—"financial responsibility"—but the whole world knows that is far too little in any case where injuries are significant. In point of fact, it is little less than irresponsible to do no more than that, as it really is every person's responsibility to make sure they can compensate those who might be injured by their negligence. And if you have minors driving your cars, that conclusion is even more obvious.

In one of our cases, a sixteen-year-old driver caused well over a million dollars in injuries when he struck two folks who were riding a motorcycle. His parents inexplicably provided only minimum coverage for him, and there was insufficient coverage even to pay the $200,000 in medical bills the plaintiffs incurred in the months following the accident. The fact that the young driver's father had failed to accept his moral obligation to adequately insure the boy was lost on him, demonstrating what an oyster he really was. If we are to drive we have to drive responsibly, and that has to include insuring ourselves in such a way as to compensate those who might be hurt by our cars. Moreover, if you do have sufficient coverage with a reputable company, the aftermath of an accident that has been your fault will be pretty inconsequential to you and your family. A few of the best known names in auto insurance have accrued well-deserved reputations for treating injured people very badly, including their own insured customers. It's no fun getting sued, but it's a lot less fun without adequate insurance. Attempting to save a few bucks on car insurance is stupid. Don't do it.

OTHER TYPES OF ACCIDENTS AND INJURIES

We were so specific in addressing automobile accident cases because they are the most frequent, and they tend to produce the most significant injuries and therefore the most litigation. What we will address now are other claims that arise out of accidents not involving cars, but the rules are the same. If you get hurt because of the neglect of someone else, whether you fall down on the ice at the mall, turn and break your ankle on the hole in the sidewalk, get bit by the neighbor's dog, or get sick from exposure to some noxious chemical, there is the potential for a recovery against those responsible. We begin with the whole concept of responsibility for keeping one's place safe.

▶Premises Liability

Students spend significant time in law school learning the many sides to this subject. Hundreds of years of cases have shaped a body of law that is, with some exceptions, very friendly toward those who enter the property of others as what the law calls either social or business "invitees." That's a way of saying you're there because they asked you to come. So when the host of the Christmas party, cookout, or cosmetics buying party fails to fix the hole in the sidewalk, clean off the snow and ice from the steps, or leaves a dangerous dog loose, there is the possibility that injuries caused by those situations will be judged as the fault of the owner. And this will produce a right to claim damages for those injuries. Most folks have premises liability coverage on their homeowners insurance policies, and *everyone* should. It's a pretty standard provision, and the cost of inclusion of that kind of coverage is worth every penny.

The bigger area of interest is the "business invitee." It's easy to understand why the law requires the most care to be exercised by those who would draw us to their places to spend money. Shopping malls, auto dealerships, medical offices, theaters, and the public streets all around them are held to the higher standard of care than the guy who has the poker party at his home on Tuesday night. We won't go through the various rules here, as it would take a whole chapter just to confuse you sufficiently so that you heave this book at the wall.

Suffice it to say that, if you are hurt because of a condition existing in a place where you go lawfully and with at least the implied invitation of the owner or occupier of the place, there may be liability for your injuries against that person. As to the world of commerce, every lease I have ever written or reviewed has had explicit requirements that made both the owner and the lessee responsible for various portions of the place, and each has to guarantee that it will maintain sufficient insurance coverage to handle injuries that might occur. Now not every slip-and-fall, turned ankle, stubbed toe, or broken manicure is fodder for a law suit, and making silly claims only drives up the cost of insurance and of doing business generally. However, you know the difference, and if you really get hurt, seek counsel quickly, and follow the rules we set out earlier.

For those readers who are instead "inviters" of the public, **GET INSURANCE!** The best way to keep your rates down and to avoid having your clients, customers, colleagues, and suppliers get hurt is to exercise great attention to the way you keep your place. Parking lot cases are always frustrating for business folks and their lawyers, because the conditions can change so quickly outside. From clear and dry to snow-covered and icy, things can turn ugly in a couple of hours. Unfortunately, the law requires great attention to such events, so keeping things safe is just a cost of doing business. And this extends to debris, potholes, spots under construction, and the like. Owners of commercial structures can even face liability for permitting conditions that let criminals prey on those who come to your buildings. Parking garages and vacant apartment buildings must be kept free of those who might attack any who are there with consent. My brother represented a young woman who had been attacked by a man who lured her to a portion of an apartment complex that was unoccupied at the time. He raped her at gunpoint, then fled. Eventually the owners paid a hefty settlement, but the woman's trauma persists today. The best way to address this kind of liability problem is to have your insurance carrier do a survey of your buildings, advising you of the things that need to be addressed to keep the public safe. Beyond the obvious problems like broken steps, uneven pavement, and loose wires or decorations, the carrier will help you deal with building security and effective evacuation preparations in the event of fire of other dangerous event.

I know this seems like excessive expense at first, but doing business means seeking the public's business—*and their money.* So it's only good business and good morality to do all you can to keep them safe while they're in your place.

▶Injuries on the Job

Most states follow the same body of law we have here in Indiana regarding work-related injuries. By statute, all employers are required to provide compensation for every worker injured while working for them. The vast majority carry workers' compensation insurance, but the statute governs even the coverage provided by those policies. Basically, the rule is that, without any consideration of fault, contributory negligence, poor judgment on either side, or other violations of law or regulation by the employer or the injured worker, the employer has to compensate the employee for all injuries incurred while on the job. That's the good news. The bad news is that the calculation of what you get for that injury is set by law, and it is a mere fraction of what the same injury might yield if not covered by comp.

The whole thing revolves around the calculation of temporary and permanent disability resulting from the injury, and that calculation is based upon the findings of a physician, usually paid by the employer. So you get paid, no matter whether you contributed to your own fate or not, but you probably will not get anything close to what the injury is worth to you in terms of loss of function, pain and suffering, and lost future income. And this statutory liability is *all* the employer has. He cannot be sued for damages in excess of that provided by workers' compensation.

It is worth consulting counsel in these cases, even though the situation may be bleak with regard to workers' compensation recovery. The lawyer can deal with the insurance company, and he or she can have you seen by a different healthcare provider, not in the employ of the boss. Sad to say, but those guys do have a remarkable tendency to find most folks far less severely injured than will the physician actually treating the problem. And even the business of determining the degree of permanent disability gets messy, as I have found that most of the occupational specialists, usually associated with industrial and occupational rehabilitation clinics in the bigger hospitals, are reluctant to go against the large employers. This is simply because they make their living seeing and evaluating injured workers employed by these concerns. Typically we have to get an occupational specialist from another community or do battle against the locals with our own medical specialists in the appropriate field, whether that be neurology, orthopedics, internal medicine, or other appropriate area. But there is more.

It may be difficult to get someone independent of the major employers in your own community to do a fresh evaluation of your comp-related injuries, as we have found repeatedly. In one recent, the physicians I contacted to evaluate my client in a different situation all refused to get involved because the defendant was a major employer in the area whose business they all either already had or were trying to get.

People who get hurt on the job are often the victims of malfunctions of equipment or design defects in machinery or structures in which they are required to operate. So if the forklift fails, the lathe flies apart, the railing gives way, or the electrical breaker system fails to save you from electric shock, there may be liability against the manufacturer, the business charged with proper maintenance, the construction contractor, or the electrician, if any of these is an outside firm. If such person is an employee of the company, there is no liability as that is covered by comp. But if he is hired to do work as an independent contractor, mistakes may lead to liability in your favor.

For example, my client was severely injured by a chemical spill that was caused by the neglect of a company hired to remove some dangerous gas from a tank on the premises of my client's employer. There was only workers' compensation available to her from the employer, but a jury found the company who made a mess of the gas removal liable for a very healthy sum. Likewise, in a case where another client's husband was killed in a forklift accident, all she got was the statutory amount permitted for death resulting from a work-related accident. But the forklift company ended up paying a significant amount to settle our claim that a design defect and improper maintenance had been the cause of his fall and resulting death on the job.

So you can see how important it is to have your case examined by competent counsel, even where your recovery from the employer is set by state law; it can make the difference between a pittance for one who is badly and permanently injured, and a full monetary recovery.

▶Medical Malpractice

The vast majority of modern healthcare providers of every description have managed to provide us with the best medical science in history, and the incidence of truly bad mistakes among them is very low. Today in the United States—and particularly in the State of Indiana—folks can count on a quality of diagnosis, treatment, and supportive care that is as good as that which exists anywhere in the world, no matter what kind of problem we face. My father began medical practice in Cumberland in the late forties, delivering babies, making house calls, setting broken bones, and sewing up lacerations for that whole community, doing pretty much whatever needed to be done to care for his people. No doubt every one of us would love to receive such personal care today, without having to scratch and claw our way through the maze of voice mail options, discourteous staff, long lines, and insurance coverage voodoo that daunts us when we seek care sometimes. But truth be known, even with its many aggravations and occasionally disagreeable moments, what we get today when we seek medical attention is a quantum leap from what Dad could do just a few years ago.

Not only is the technology beyond comparison, but the medical professionals who care for us are the best trained, most experienced and committed (with occasional exceptions) people to be found. It is a rare physician who really drops the ball because he just doesn't care what happens; they are fine scientists and superb clinicians in nearly every case. But we all know of the horror stories where bad errors have been made, with catastrophic results for the patient. For purposes of our coverage here, it is those uncommon but awful results that are of concern.

The typical medical malpractice case does not include the egregious screw-ups like amputating the wrong leg, killing the patient with the wrong medication, or blowing an obvious diagnosis. What happens to put a healthcare provider on the wrong side of civil liability is making an error in judgment or performance of procedure or delivery of care.

According to the 2000 Indiana Legal Education Forum Medical Malpractice Manual, "A physician must exercise that degree of care, skill and proficiency exercised by reasonably careful, skillful and prudent practitioners in the same class to which he or she belongs, acting under the same or similar circumstances. . . . A hospital is responsible for the negligent acts of its employees which are done within the scope of their employment."

One who is injured or made sick by the physician's violation of that prevailing standard of care has two years from the date of the incidence of such error in which to bring a claim. This rule may at times be altered when the condition takes longer than that to appear, such as the situation where the damage done by the provider produces a delayed reaction—one that fails to become symptomatic for a time after the error is committed. This also is true when the doctor or other professional hides the evidence of the malpractice, concealing wrongdoing.

The case is commenced by the filing of a proposed complaint that sets out the claim with the Indiana Department of Insurance; the department then starts a really arduous process that includes notifying the defendant and his carrier and establishing a "medical review panel" that will review the case. The parties select a panel chairman and then submit names of physicians who will actually review the case as a panel. Here is where the injustice of the whole game is evident, as the insurance companies often continue to object to the plaintiff's proposed panel members for one reason or another, causing the case to languish for months or a year *or more* before getting under way.

A few years ago a physician in an emergency room of a local hospital blew an obvious diagnosis on an elderly client of ours, and as the result of that error, our otherwise healthy, independent senior lost all the vision in her one good eye. We filed the necessary paperwork, but the other side screwed with the process for so long our client had finally died before the matter could be completed. We finally got as far as having a panel selected, and the case was submitted for decision. No surprise, notwithstanding our top-notch medical expert and obvious injuries, the medical review panel ruled against us. We filed suit, but the whole thing collapsed with her death. I still wonder how those guys sleep at night, employing such tactics.

Both sides submit their medical reports, records, and expert opinions, and usually without the taking of oral testimony, the panel makes a determination whether or not the care provided met the standard of care. And while no one likes to lose his or her case before the medical review panel, even if that happens, the plaintiff can still file suit after this process is complete.

It is easy to see why having experienced counsel is a must. Not every personal injury lawyer does malpractice work, so that is one more item for your checklist, as the vagaries and aggravations of winding through the review panel process are a real pain in the backside. Damages under the statute are capped by statute, and at printing of this book that figure is $1,250,000. Punitive damages are not permitted, but if the defendant has not qualified under the Indiana malpractice law, the caps do not apply. The lawyers will know how to determine whether or not the doctor in question is so qualified.

With all that accomplished, the case eventually proceeds like other accident cases, with the parties working to establish damages, permanent impairment, disfigurement, and the like. Unfortunately settlement is often more difficult, as the defendants fight payment for reasons that don't apply to negligent drivers or landlords. There is a nationwide database into which are reported the results of all malpractice claims, and that information stays with that provider. So you can see that this minefield is not for the faint-of-heart or the novice. Expect the case to last longer and cost more than other claims might, and be prepared for a major dose of exasperation before it is concluded.

▶Products Liability

This area has to do with things we buy that fail to work as they are supposed to. Obviously the lawnmower, car, truck, dishwasher, computer, fishing rod, or garage door opener that doesn't work is immediately the subject of a warranty claim back to the guy from whom the purchase was made. Consumer issues are addressed in a later chapter, but for now we are interested in products that fail to perform as they are supposed to and which, in failing, cause injury. This is at times complicated stuff, so what you should get from this discussion is enough information to recognize whether or not you should seek counsel to determine if a claim exists.

If you are injured in an automobile accident, the whole debate over who was at fault in causing the wreck is central. But when the brakes fail, the power steering quits, the tires fly apart, or the gas tank explodes on impact, other targets for liability may appear. Now keep in mind: *simple mechanical failures do not necessarily yield fault on the part of the manufacturer.* Nothing lasts forever, and things like brake and tire failures occur naturally over time, particularly if the owner or operator fails to properly maintain the vehicle. But in instances such as the infamous Ford exploding gas tanks and disintegrating Firestone tires, the issue of manufacturer liability arises. If you are hurt in an accident and there is evidence of some kind of mechanical failure or some system error that contributed to the accident or to the injuries sustained, it's time to tell the lawyer about it. For example, one whose injuries are the result of an air bag system that failed to deploy on impact or an exhaust system that, due to design defect or defect in fabrication or installation, leaked carbon monoxide into the passenger cabin, may have a claim against those who were responsible for it. That will usually be the manufacturer, but courts have also found liability against after-market installers of components and service or repair providers.

There are many other areas of potential liability in this field, from exploding soft-drink bottles to defective exercise equipment. We had one case where a fast-food restaurant served our client a beverage that contained a chunk of plastic that had come off the device that made the semi-frozen drink. It was just the right size to get as far as the guy's windpipe, but not big enough to pass on out of the way, and his life was saved only by quick work on the part of his wife. However, he was comatose for a time, and the damages were fairly substantial. If you get hurt because of such an occurrence, the best thing to do is to save all the parts, take pictures if appropriate, and seek counsel. It is often the case that folks fail to realize how badly they have been hurt until after the telltale artifacts are gone.

▶ Wrongful Death

Loss of a life is never trivial, and losing a loved one due to the neglect of another is particularly bitter. The law recognizes the intrinsic value of life by statute, and a number of rules apply that only the lawyer in the particular situation can adequately explain. Unfortunately, the aspects of untimely death that most hurt those who are left behind are really not addressed well by Indiana law. Essentially, the law recognizes the value of those who are killed by the wrongful conduct of others mostly in economic terms. So the forty-year-old father of three, earning $100,000 per year who was also caring for his mother and three disabled siblings, may be worth a significant amount in damages under the statute, but the five-year-old lost to an auto accident will have none of those attributes to push up the value of the loss. It all sounds crass and brutal, but "facts are facts." More recently, the law has become a bit more attentive to those who lose someone not in the breadwinner category. However, you should be aware that our law still places the greater value on those whose death spells economic hardship for their dependents than on those whose departure simply leaves a horrible gaping hole in the lives of those who must go on without them. All the before-mentioned rules apply, no matter how the wrongful death occurred, so get busy finding counsel and keeping records without delay.

The only party who can bring an action in Indiana for wrongful death is the person appointed by the court as personal representative of the estate. Even where there are no physical assets, or where the assets are insufficient to merit opening a probate estate, one must be opened for the purpose of prosecuting the action. The parties who get the benefit of whatever recovery is realized are the dependents of the deceased person, as they are the ones who lost their source of support when the decedent died. We were involved in one case where the decedent was murdered. We brought an action on behalf of the mother who was being supported by the deceased son, but in the end the mother of an illegitimate child won out as the personal representative. And because the child was the primary dependent of the dead man, she ended up controlling the litigation and reaping the lion's share of the settlement proceeds.

It's a tough spot for sure, and the emotional ingredients only make things more difficult yet, but my experience in these cases is that they are worth pursuing, unless the baseline issues of fault and resulting liability are absent. But just like with criminal prosecutions for homicide, the end results are only partially satisfying; nothing brings back the lost life.

CHAPTER TWO
⚖ Domestic Relations

I F POLITICS IS THE SCIENCE OF THE POSSIBLE, THEN THE AREA WE CALL domestic relations or Family Law must be the alchemy of the impossible, so full of confounding and unknowable issues has it become. Dominated by the divorce law with all its contentious subtopics and attempts at uniformity, it is at best a flawed answer to the arcane and even the ridiculous. But Family Law, so named because of its treatment of a variety of relationships and problems that affect the basic building block of American society, addresses much more than divorce, custody, property, and money.

We explore in these pages issues relating to adoption and abuse, education of the young, and protection of those exposed to harm in a number of ways. And I am unfortunately confident as we begin that you will finish these pages less than satisfied with the efforts of modern domestic relations law to deal with all these issues. However, be certain of this: In human interrelationship there are no equations, balanced or otherwise, to describe or to repair damage and loss that accompanies the anguish we suffer in divorce, death, injury, or the commission of crime. This effort by our legislature and our courts is, while far from perfect, a true yeoman's work product, and the mechanisms they have put in place provide the only predictable and workable solutions to some of life's most complex and difficult problems.

DIVORCE

I know a lot more about this subject than I wish I did, having been involved in divorce cases for over twenty-five years; I have also been divorced—*twice*—so the subject is one with which I am well familiar, both as lawyer and client. We spend no time here moralizing over whether or not divorce is a good thing, for in point of fact, it is a reality in our society. And although I subscribe to the thesis that God intended us to marry well and for life, mankind has had less than the best luck with that particular injunction from the Almighty. Apparently somewhere between a third and half of all those who get married will have to face the misery of a divorce, so we will simply accept that fact and address the law as it guides Hoosiers through the difficult terrain that ends in a dissolved marriage after one quick admonition:

A relationship is a tricky thing on a good day, and the presence of children, money problems, booze, infidelities of many kinds, and the pressures of all that life can dump on us only serve to make marriage more difficult at times. Do yourself the favor of counting to ten—or ten thousand—before pulling the trigger on the whole thing. Your temper, your hurt feelings, even your best friend's advice, can get in the way of making decisions from which there may be no return, so consider carefully, prayerfully, repeatedly, what you decide to do. Kids survive and bounce back for sure, but never doubt that, in the vast majority of cases, they would far prefer that Mom and Dad stay together. Family is almost always better than no family. Just think long and hard first; do not let the moment dictate a lifetime decision.

In Indiana, we do just five main things when people decide to divorce. The courts dissolve their marriage, divide their property, establish custody over their children, provide for support for those children until they are emancipated, make provision for them to share time with both their parents, and in appropriate but unusual cases, grant spousal maintenance for folks who cannot care for themselves after the marriage is dissolved. The marriage gets dissolved simply by the decree of the court declaring that the marriage is ended. But from there on, the rules are more complex, so we will address them in order.

▶ Division of Property

We view Indiana marriages as producing a "one pot" of marital assets, which include, presumptively, everything a couple possesses on the date they first separate from each other. The statute establishes a presumption that the parties will evenly divide their assets, after taking into account any liabilities (debts) that exist at the time of division. In the vast majority of cases, this will mean just what it says—each side will get about half the property of the marriage, after allowance for debt accumulated during the time the parties were married and living together. *There are a large number of exceptions and other wrinkles in this body of law, but what we provide here are the general rules under the statute and case law that govern the area.* Having established this presumption of equal division of property, the statute then sets out a number of criteria that are to be applied by the courts in deciding whether or not to deviate from this presumption. They are as follows:

1. Contribution by each spouse, regardless of whether the contribution was "income-producing"

2. The extent to which property was acquired by either spouse before the marriage or by inheritance or gift

3. The economic circumstance of either spouse at the time of division, including in that determination the needs of a spouse with custody of minor children to have possession of the marital residence

4. The ways in which either party has disposed of or dissipated marital assets during the marriage

5. Earnings and earning abilities of each party.

As you can see, this list of factors can cut both ways—often at the same time. And it is this list of exceptions to the presumption of equal division that typically keeps the courts resting in the safe harbor of that presumption. The Court of Appeals doesn't like much deviation, unless the evidence is strong in support of it, so expect the courts to carve things down the middle most of the time. The issues that can be most significant to the court in deviating from an even split typically include big differences in the income potential of the parties and evidence of marital misconduct that has cost the estate significantly.

We represented a wife whose husband had had a long-term girlfriend on whom he had expended thousands of marital dollars without his wife's knowledge or consent. The guy even admitted to the judge that he had done so, and the court was quick to exact a price for that misconduct. Basically, the court simply called what he had wasted on his true love part of his portion of the estate, and our client got the rest. Anyone who has wasted the estate on wild living can expect to suffer the court's wrath when it comes time to make a division. To the contrary, however, in cases where the marriage has been short, and the contributions much greater by one side than the other, expect the bigger contributor to be recognized as such. Note that there is built into this whole statutory scheme a method of recognizing the contributions of those who manage and keep a home and raise kids. In long marriages, with kids born and raised and wealth accumulated, expect that Mom's worst day in court is the old 50/50 presumption. My old friend Jim Buck, the guy who pretty much broke me into this business in the first place and who is a superb advocate in this difficult area, once told me that the bigger the estate, the less likely the court will be to deviate very much from the presumed even division. The lawyer will have to examine all these factors to give you good advice here.

▶Spousal Maintenance

This area is sticky, and the courts dislike it with just cause. The idea of keeping people financially connected to each other beyond child support is inconsistent with the whole concept of divorce, and the courts require serious proof of a real and provably disabling condition before saddling one of the parties with financial responsibility for the other after the marriage is dissolved. Maintenance for a spouse after the divorce has been concluded can be awarded by the court where that spouse has demonstrated a real inability to provide for his or her own care in the future. Those maintenance payments are deductible to the payer and taxable to the recipient, and they do not constitute a part of the division of the property of the marriage. They are in addition to it. Cases where a spouse actually gets this kind of award are uncommon; I've been in this business for twenty-eight years, and I've only been involved in a small handful of cases where the issue was serious enough to take up the court's time. Moreover, if the parties have significant assets, judges are unlikely to want to hit one side with additional responsibilities where the party seeking maintenance will recover a sizable estate upon division of property anyway. One rule of thumb here might be that the bigger the net estate share going to the disabled party, the less likely the court will be to consider maintenance very seriously. Suffice it to say that the party seeking such assistance needs to have a strong case for it, complete with medical support that is specific and compelling, and a lawyer who is competent to make the case well in court.

▶Child Custody

What a mess. In twenty-eight years I have been involved in hundreds of cases where arguments over who would get the kids have been a part of the fabric of the proceeding. Of those, we have actually tried fewer than fifty as contested cases where custody was actually litigated. The ones where one parent was a drunk, an addict, a crook, or just plain no good, have been easy, and trying them was seldom necessary. In the rest of the cases, the real problem has seldom been what the statute declares as the main idea, that of the "best interests of the children." More often the parties make hockey pucks out of the kids because of their own issues, their own confusion at such difficult times, and often just their own bitter animus toward the estranged spouse.

Even in the most clear-cut cases, people get silly and avoid obvious and rational solutions to their problems. While no one really doubts where the kids should be, they'll fight over it for a while anyway, avoiding the obvious right answer, sometimes for many months, before finally finishing things appropriately. Call it some kind of emotional or psychological convalescence or just a well-deserved but attenuated tantrum, it has to pass, no matter how it is labeled. **But be clear on this: the sooner the parties can put the past into perspective and set aside their venom toward each other, the** sooner the case will end and life can begin anew. **AND THE KIDS WILL IN NO EVENT BEGIN TO HEAL FROM THE WOUNDS THEY HAVE SUFFERED UNTIL THAT MARITAL WARFARE IS FINISHED.** One of the best Indiana practitioners in this area, Bruce Pennamped, has often asked clients in the throes of this mess whether or not they wanted to decide what would happen to their kids and property or if they would prefer to have some stranger do it for them. Good question, Bruce, for that is what happens with those who refuse to deal with their own divorce issues. *Growing up is hard to do, but the adults are the ones who must lead the way.*

As we will also see in the area of computation of child support, custody/visitation issues are becoming more and more the subject of guidelines promulgated by the Indiana Supreme Court. For many years each county has had a set of guidelines addressing issues of parental visitation with minor children, and although there were variations between counties, most of their provisions were similar. Recently, the courts have adopted a statewide set of "Parenting Time Guidelines," a framework in which to provide some consistency throughout the state. And although these guidelines do not specifically deal with custody, they are liberal and broad enough that, once the bench and bar get accustomed to the new vocabulary, I think those new things will promote earlier and fairer resolution in many cases. When the old "who gets the kids" bright line gets more blurred, so that neither side is typically faced with "giving up the kids" to the other, egos and emotions will play a lesser role in the whole thing. However, there are a few truisms about this messy area that might be of use here:

1. Moms still get primary physical custody of the kids more often than not; especially when children are small and the mom has been the primary caregiver before the divorce was filed. My own lawyer, Doug Church, calls this the "biological imperative," and that's pretty close. Dads who want to challenge that one need to have a strong case for rebutting the traditional view.

2. Dads who have not been involved seriously in their kids' lives before the divorce is filed cannot expect to get cus-

tody awards. Disneyland dads don't impress judges.

3. Anyone who has demonstrated emotional or psychological traits that might be dangerous or undesirable for the kids to deal with can expect to lose the custody battle. This goes for moms as well as dads, and just like in kindergarten it's still best to keep your hands—and your big mouth—to yourself.

4. Kids typically go with the house. This is not hard and fast, and there are frequent exceptions to it, but there is something attractive about minimizing the disruption of the kids' lives by the family breakup. Of course, where the house is too much for either spouse to maintain and pay for after the divorce is final, this does not apply, but expect the court to do what it can to keep these disruptions to a reasonable minimum.

5. Exposing children during the time the case is pending to new romantic interests is bad policy. Period. Not only is it confusing and disheartening to them, judges don't like it. Moreover, case law in Indiana tells us that "cohabitation" with a romantic interest outside of marriage (we used to call that "shacking up") may be cause for limiting visitation or even changing custody. Sounds old-fashioned, but the courts still frown on exposing the kids to that kind of conduct. This is not to say a court will so rule, but the case law tells us that a court that makes a determination that exposure to cohabitation is not in the kids' best interest will not be likely to get reversed on appeal.

6. Unless one of the parties is really bad news where the kids are concerned, it's stupid to fight over custody. The law requires that the "non-primary" custodian of the children must be the first-choice sitter, that they get half the summer and every other holiday, in addition to regular weeknight and weekend time. With that kind of presumed result after most fights, the idea of spending thousands of dollars on lawyers and so-called custody experts is truly a

fool's errand. For example, where the "non-primary custodian" has every other weekend from Friday evening through Sunday evening, dinner one night a week, and half the summer, that parent will see the children about 130 to 140 days a year, or just under half the days. Add to that spring break, fall break, Christmas/New Year's break, alternating holidays and birthdays, and the number of days becomes very equal, even though not all those days include overnight stays. Work it out yourself. Recently the estranged husband of one of my clients became fixated on "having equal time" with the kids. His guilt over his extra-marital escapades, in my view, was the primary motivation for all this newfound passion, but he was stuck on it. His children suffered terribly while he continued to make the world, his wife, and even me, the enemy, before finally discovering that he needed to think of the kids first.

7. Most psychologists who do evaluation work for the courts are no better at figuring out the answers than a judge would be without their input. With a few notable exceptions, these people end up dividing the baby, hedging their bets in favor of the middle of the road, and leaving the parties no closer to a conclusion than they were before the process began. This kind of report can cost as much as five to six thousand dollars—money the parties have to pay out of the marital pot. Recently my experience has been that the evaluator appeared to agree with *everyone*, failing to separate the rat droppings from the black pepper, and the report was a pure study in tepidness. So just remember, it's expensive, time-consuming, frustrating, and often productive of no more insight than you should have brought to the table yourself.

8. "Getting even," or other such juvenile attitudes, is best left in junior high. It's not moral, it's not honest, and it doesn't work. My associate attempted to get a case mediated recently, and the opposing client was so full of vengeance and rage, so consumed with self and hatred for

the other side, that the whole thing was an exercise in futility. It cost this person over a thousand dollars in fees and mediation costs, and the mediator finally threw in the towel after declaring that the angry party was impossible to reason with. And when that behavior is centered on custody/visitation issues, you can make book that that same poison pervades the household and batters the children constantly.

9. Remember the kids, because they pay most of the bills. You may write checks, give up property, even agree to pick up contested debt, but they pay the real currency in human terms. So recognize that fact quickly and come to a conclusion that takes them out of the arena. Besides, whatever you finally agree on will change over time. They grow up, get drivers' licenses, and eventually go off to school, so nothing is forever anyway.

Under Indiana law, after the age of fourteen the desires of the child become very important. The statute lists a number of points that will be relevant, and that includes "the wishes of the child, with more consideration given to the child's wishes if the child is at least fourteen years of age." This leads us back to the common sense conclusion. With older kids and two reasonably good parents, there is no reason to battle over the fine print on a custody/parenting time deal. The sooner we grow up and come to an ordered conclusion the sooner we stop spending money and punishing the kids for our failures. Think about it.

▶Child Support

This is, with few exceptions, now an arithmetic exercise in Indiana. A state guideline determines the amount to be paid, takes into account shared custody arrangements, split custody, college, and special needs. The guidelines determine, based upon pretty extensive research, a figure that should be appropriate for the given number of kids at every income level from poverty to great wealth. The incomes of both sides are added together, then that number is used to find a gross support figure on the chart. Whatever that number is, the worksheet applies the percentage of income contributed by each side to that figure, and the result is support to be paid by that parent who is "non-primary" under the custody arrangement. Where parenting time is pretty even, the court will include that in this calculation. There are provisions for taking into account who provides medical coverage, how the parties are to divide uninsured expenses, what to do during the summer and at other times when the kids are with that parent for extended periods, and how to handle college. Again, I am continually amazed by parents, particularly fathers who can afford to do it, who spend so much time arguing over caring for their own children. Moms must expect, if they are working at all, to contribute to college on the same ratio of payment that is used to calculate support, and dads have to expect to pay a portion of uninsured medical expenses whether or not they provide insurance. More detail here will just confuse things, but expect to pay your proportionate share of the costs of raising and educating your children, and expect the calculation of those contributions to be pretty cut-and-dried.

▶Modification

The whole idea of getting divorced is to have things finished, and the decree that a court enters at the end of the proceeding is intended in large measure to do just that. The marriage is dissolved, the property divided, former names restored if requested, and fees ordered paid. Those features of the decree are essentially set in stone, not to be revisited except in rare circumstances. But child custody, support, and post-decree spousal maintenance are specifically exempt from that list, as the court retains what is called "continuing jurisdiction" over the parties for those purposes. So when Mom claims that the support has become insufficient in light of increased expenses and increases in Dad's income, she can "go back to court" to seek an increase. Likewise, where one side believes that the existing custody arrangement has ceased to be in the children's best interests, the court will hear evidence and make a determination about requests for a change there, too. The same holds true where spousal maintenance has been ordered; the court addresses both the amount and the actual continuation of payments. In all cases where either side thinks changes should be made, the courts can be expected to rely on experts very heavily, particularly in matters dealing with custody. It is a heavy burden to bear when one tries to get a court to change a status quo, so having strong evidence and competent counsel experienced in such matters is crucial. The best thing to do here is to work very hard at resolving the matter without going back at all. Custody changes are more often than not related to the changes in the kids as they grow up, and again, the older the kids get, the more their wishes weigh in the decision. Before I swore off ever doing another one, I tried custody cases over everything from parental drug abuse to abandonment to parents who decided to move their true love in with the kids—but without benefit of a marriage license. The court had no trouble granting Dad custody in the case where he kept finding the kids on the street corner after Mom had gone off to score some heroin. There was no trouble getting another father custody when Mom moved the fourth boyfriend in six months into the apartment with her eleven-year-old daughter. And things were pretty easy as well when another mom simply took off for sunny California to reunite with her high school flame. However, scores of other cases were less clear, and the expense and misery factors were huge every time.

ADOPTION

It may sound like I have become a broken record here, but the most important thing to remember about this tender area is having a lawyer who knows how to get the job done. It is easy to find a child to adopt if you are prepared to deal with older kids, special needs or abused kids, or others who many often characterize as less desirable, but finding a newborn whose background and ethnicity matches that of the parents is a bigger order. However, the state is full of children who desperately need a home, and anyone who wants to be a parent and can qualify to do so, can really have adoptive children in his or her home in a short time. We will not go through the many options and all the technicalities here, but just be aware that no adoption can proceed without court approval and a decree that makes the child the legal "offspring" of the adoptive parents. This will necessarily entail a welfare home study, submission of detailed and complete personal and professional information about you, and a demonstration that you have the financial wherewithal to provide for a child.

There are many agencies in Indiana that provide adoption services, including locating children who fit the desires of the parents and taking care of the business of interviews and the like. One can also do what is called a private placement, where foster parents or an expectant mother are connected with a couple seeking a child. In that case, a welfare investigation and interview process is still done, but there is no agency involvement. In all cases, placement is approved and adoption decreed by a court with the appropriate jurisdiction. In most counties, that is the Circuit or Superior Court, except in those few counties where there is a probate court that handles all adoptions. If you seek adoption, the first place to go is not the court or the lawyer, but the agency, unless you have found a child you wish to adopt. In that case, the lawyer is the first stop, and those who know what they are doing will take it from there. An expectant mother who expresses her desire to relinquish her rights and permit adoption immediately after birth signs forms and submits to study, as do the prospective adoptive parents, and getting all this detail handled quickly and accurately at once will do much to avoid problems when the child is born.

Of course, if an adoption is to occur, the rights of the biological parents will have to be terminated, unless those persons are deceased. There are numerous provisions for termination of parental rights under Indiana law, including termination by consent, upon proof of unfitness that is also accompanied by a court finding and decree to that effect, and failure to support the child. This can be a very technical area, one full of input by and control from state and local agencies. Suffice it to say here that, if you are interested in attempting adoption of a child whose parents are living but who have failed to care for the child, have abused the child, or have abandoned the child, you will have to follow specific procedures and follow the directions of the courts. It is clearly worth it, and one should not be dissuaded from the mission by the presence of some paperwork. Despite the occasional horror story to the contrary, the vast majority of agencies and courts are eager to help kids get away from harm and into the best possible environment.

CHAPTER THREE
⚖ Criminal Law

T HE CRIMINAL LAW IS DIVIDED INTO CATEGORIES OF VIOLATIONS UNDER A code of statutes, both state and federal. The smallest or most innocuous of them are called infractions, and they include parking tickets, simple speeding violations, and things like noisy dogs and leaky mufflers. From infractions we move to misdemeanors, of which there are three classes, and those include a wide array of charges for misconduct more serious than infractions, but less important than felonies. Misdemeanors as most people might encounter them include the more serious traffic offenses like reckless driving and first drunk-driving offenses, simple assault, possession of controlled substances in small quantities where there is no implication of sale or other delivery, and certain property crimes. On this list are things like criminal mischief, criminal conversion, and the old "common nuisance" charges. Then there are felonies, crimes that require intent and that carry potential prison sentences of more than a year. What we will concentrate on here will be those areas most likely to become of importance to the average Hoosier.

DRUNK DRIVING

Many a sad defendant has heard his lawyer say that it would be easier to beat a bank robbery charge or sale of cocaine than to get past a drunk-driving rap, and in many ways they are right. Every legislator, candidate for governor, attorney general, or prosecutor seems to feel the need to talk tougher than the guy before him when it comes to throwing the book at those who are charged with driving while under the influence. Now don't get me wrong—drunks kill thousands of people every year, and punishing them while getting them off the road is extremely important stuff. However, there are a few realities that face the defendant charged with that offense that bear discussion here, and the first is understanding just how appealing it is for law enforcement, prosecutors, and judges to come crashing down on those who face such a fate.

The concept is pretty simple: one who is caught operating a motor vehicle at a time when his blood contains at least .08% alcohol is guilty of at least a Class C misdemeanor (it's a Class A misdemeanor if the blood alcohol is .15% or higher), whether or not there is evidence of intoxication aside from the test itself. Those of us who have prosecuted such charges know that such a rule makes things pretty easy for the state. Just introduce the test results from the breathalyzer into evidence and you've accomplished the mission. It's not quite that simple, but with the way the statute is written now, that's pretty close. The problem with the whole concept of proving this type of case by means of a device that measures the percentage of alcohol in the blood of the person is that there are so many variables that go into that equation. Once upon a time it was necessary for the prosecution to prove that a person so charged had also demonstrated some kind of erratic driving behavior that supported the test findings. That is no longer the case. If you get pulled over, take the test, and blow a .08, you're it. There is also the charge of "Driving while intoxicated," which requires proof of more than just the test result, but such a conviction also results in a Class C misdemeanor, unless one endangers another by his driving behavior. Then it becomes a Class A misdemeanor. Here are a few of those variables:

1. Body weight is a significant ingredient in the intoxication equation. Bigger people can generally hold more alcohol than smaller people can. It is the theory that, no matter the body weight, if a person has drunk enough booze to get to .08, he or she is under the influence, but it just takes more to get the bigger guy over the top. Forensic toxicologists will argue all over the place on this one, some towing the party line, others claiming that their testing shows a different result. Bigger people, they claim,

may be less impaired at .08 than the smaller folks are. The rule of thumb has always been that the human body could metabolize a drink per hour, whether that is defined as one beer, a six-ounce glass of wine, or one ounce of distilled spirits.

2. The baseline of .08 means different things to different defendants. There are plenty of studies that show a wide variation of impairment in people whose tested blood alcohol is at that level. Is the person who demonstrates good motor control, diction, and demeanor, but who tests .08, "driving while under the influence?" Clearly not, but he's just as guilty as the guy who's crawling on his knees and speaking in tongues.

3. There is a battery of field sobriety tests given to people suspected of being under the influence when they are stopped and the police officer believes they might be over the limit. These include some moves that are pretty tricky, especially at night, and even more so when it's really cold outside. Walking heel-to-toe, standing at attention and touching the end of the nose, and following the cop's finger as it is moved in front of the subject's face are all a part of this drill. (One of our clients, a man who was of small stature, was required to perform these tests in ten-degree weather, at a time when he was wearing no winter coat. Obviously he failed.) Failing to perform well on these items lands the subject in the back of the patrol car, headed for a location where there is a breathalyzer machine.

4. After one consumes his last drink of the evening, his blood alcohol will continue to go up for a period of at least an hour. This is because the body continues to absorb and metabolize the booze over time after the person has quit drinking. That may explain why you feel worse by the time you go to bed than you did when you left the party! In any event, where the defendant is arrested shortly after leaving the restaurant, party or bar, he or she may be fine, but will smell of alcohol. During the intervening hour

that passes between the moment of arrest and the administration of the test, the old blood alcohol goes up appreciably as the body is absorbing that last drink. Was the guy under the influence when stopped? Maybe not, but he almost certainly will be the unhappy recipient of the .08 award by the time he gets to the station for testing. *Here is one of the few really meaningful defenses that sometimes work in these cases. If your lawyer can prove how much you had to drink during the evening by the testimony of others who were with you, a toxicologist testifying for you can estimate what your blood alcohol would have been at the time of arrest, knowing what it was an hour later.* It's a bit of a long shot, but it's worked for us, and the science behind the defense is very reliable.

5. The way you behave makes a huge difference. The driver who gets pulled over for some traffic infraction or a missing taillight and who has consumed enough alcohol to smell like it can do something to avoid making things worse. Being courteous, producing required information quickly and without difficulty, and complying with initial requests by the officer will go a long way toward forming the impression of your physical state. Arguing, cracking wise, and demonstrating irritation or belligerence are all equally sure—and stupid—ways of encouraging evermore intense interest in your behavior. In point of fact, such conduct so often accompanies the intoxicated driver that most officers will decide they've landed a live one every time such nonsense occurs. And anyone—*ANYONE*—who tries to get physical, attempts to leave the scene of the traffic stop, or commits the cardinal sin of swearing at the cop, is a dead duck. The defense lawyer may have all kinds of esoteric arguments to make about your body weight, drinking habits, and earlier consumption that night, and even some wonderful proof of your saintly reputation as a community icon, but if you've acted like an idiot at the scene, you're toast. No judge will tolerate such behavior toward the police, and the moment that officer starts talking about having to subdue the defendant, call for back-

up, take the keys from the defendant's car, or tolerate dirty talk, it's over. The judge's eyes may glaze over, his attention wander, and his resolution become clear—and you won't like the result.

6. Most defenses to drunk driving charges don't work. Simply put, they fail because most folks arrested for that charge are guilty, and the proof is hardly rocket science. Judges who hear these cases hear them by the ton, are wise to the usual defenses, and are probably personally familiar with the cops testifying. *A note here: in this whole criminal law area, this holds true. Those who shoulder the daunting task of adjudicating such cases, from traffic violations to capital murder, quickly lose the capacity to indulge in fiction, fantasy, or novel theories. Being a criminal court judge is among the most difficult assignments a judge can ever assume, and the resulting cynicism that comes from watching humankind at its worst every day creates a filter that weeds out most defense tactics.* Everyone knows the old adage that says "if it moves like a duck, quacks like a duck, and looks like a duck, it's probably a duck." Well, if you look, act, and sound like a drunk, all the king's horses and all the king's men will have a difficult time convincing one of these folks that you were really just on your knees in the parking lot searching for the back to your wife's diamond earring.

▶*Negotiated Pleas in Drunk-Driving Cases*

I go back to the same advice as always here regarding counsel. And I do so not just because defending these charges takes experience and familiarity with the law, but because the vast majority of such cases are resolved by a plea. The lawyer familiar with the courts, the cops, and the practices of the local prosecutor regarding drunk driving will be capable of working out the best arrangement, one that impacts your ability to drive and work in the least painful way.

These days the judge, although the final arbiter in every case, typically follows the recommendations of the prosecutor. And the prosecutors in most counties of Indiana have put together guidelines and programs that deal with most every description of case in this category, from first offenders to career traffic offender charges. Here is where the knowledgeable lawyer is crucial. For many who find themselves facing an alcohol-related charge for the first time, there are pretrial arrangements that permit pleas to lesser charges, limited retention of driving privileges, and even ultimate dismissal of the case after completion by the defendant of certain require- ments. We are not aware of any prosecutors who will actually permit one of these "pretrial diversion" results on a drunk-driving case, but the rules do not prohibit doing so. These may include alcohol treat- ment or counseling, community service, or a short jail sentence. The first-time offender whose charges do not include causing an accident, hurting someone, or getting stupid with the police can hope for a better deal than the repeat offender whose case includes really bad conduct.

▶ Penalties for Drunk Driving

Here are the possible results for those charged with driving under the influence in Indiana:

1. Persons convicted of driving with a blood alcohol of at least .08% but less than .15% commit a Class C misde- meanor.

2. Persons convicted of driving with a blood alcohol of .15% or more commit a Class A misdemeanor.

3. Those who are convicted of "driving while intoxicated" commit a Class C misdemeanor.

4. If the defendant is convicted of "driving while intoxi- cated" and also of having endangered another person in doing so, it is a Class A misdemeanor.

5. Where there is a charge of driving while having a blood alcohol of at least .08 and there is a prior conviction within the past five years for driving while intoxicated, the of- fense is a Class D felony.

In all these cases, the statute now provides for a mandatory suspension of driving privileges of at least ninety days. The rules are complicated and lengthy, so we will not review them here, but suffice it to say, a loss of license is a given where the defendant is convicted at all. Provisions are present for restricted license arrangements, but even those are subject to an initial mandatory suspension. Almost nobody goes to jail for drunk driving in Indiana, at least not the first time, unless other misconduct or an accident has been involved. But those subsequent offense convictions, particularly those that are class D felonies, can be expected to provide for a short vacation as the guest of the county. Any person who has sustained a conviction for one of these offenses must decide to change his or her driving and drinking habits forever. The consequence of landing in jail is most unpleasant.

DRUG CHARGES

Everything I know about illegal controlled substances tells me the whole problem represents a sad commentary on modern life in America. Whether you or someone else is charged with some little misdemeanor possession or with actual delivery of a major league bad substance like cocaine or heroin, the crime committed is not to be minimized or ignored. Remember that every conviction for a drug-related offense carries a significant stigma that follows the defendant like a bad penny. Job applications, bonding for some sensitive forms of employment, and the like all get messy when one is required to disclose prior drug-related misconduct. And make no mistake, even what many young folks consider "harmless grass" possession can and often does produce unintended and bitter fruit years after the fact. Now the trouble needs to be avoided in the first place, as I have attempted to tell many a young scholar over the years, but if one ends up facing charges, there are some important facts and details that must be recognized:

1. There are programs for pretrial disposition of misdemeanor cases involving possession of marijuana in many counties. These require attendance at various counseling

sessions, community service work, and sometimes short jail sentences, but all typically result in an ultimate dismissal of charges if the defendant is successful in completing the requirements and also staying out of trouble—usually for at least a year.

2. Where no delivery of an illegal controlled substance is involved, jail sentences for first-time offenders are rare. The jails are just too full to house non-violent defendants who have no history of drug abuse or trafficking. A lawyer who is familiar with the policies of the local prosecutor can usually accomplish a disposition that minimizes the class of crime to which the person must plead guilty and also avoid jail time as well.

3. If the person charged with possession, even of a small amount of a substance like marijuana, has prior convictions for drug-related offenses of any kind, the whole game changes immediately. The programs available do not permit repeat offenders to qualify for preferred pretrial disposition, and statutory provisions for enhanced sentences start to kick in.

▶Drug Dealing and Transporting

For those who get sucked into the outrageously stupid world of drug dealing at any level, the realities are all unwelcome, to say the least. More likely, they are just plain ugly. If you have been caught selling or transporting drugs, *no matter what they may be,* all bets are off, and the only way out of real time in the pokey is to play ball with the cops. And this means juveniles as well as adults. Expect to become the undercover assistant to the local or state narcotics officers. This will mean identifying sources, setting up controlled purchases, wearing a wire, and often testifying in court against those you help get arrested. Sound like fun? The point is anything but fun, but is painfully clear: messing around, even casually, with the delivery of *any* controlled substance, regardless of what it is and the quantity involved, is a really bad idea. I have seen defendants as young as sixteen years old wired up and sent in to purchase from their sources while the police sat outside listening to the whole thing happen.

We will address the differences among the various classes of felonies later, but an important fact to remember right now is that it takes a pretty small amount of the more dangerous drugs to land a person in the penitentiary for a long time. For example, the highest degree of felony under our criminal code is the Class A felony, carrying with it a presumptive prison term of not less than thirty years. It takes delivery of just three grams of cocaine, or about a tenth of an ounce, to make a Class A felony, and the prisons are full of dummies who got caught doing just that. Even possession of lesser quantities of cocaine constitutes a Class C felony, and the sentences there range from two to eight years. The same holds true for heroin, methamphetamine, LSD, and other major drugs in the illicit trade inventory. Only marijuana requires more bulk to make the big leagues, with delivery of ten pounds or more being a Class C felony. The problem with grass cases is that the cops are always interested in the bigger quantities, especially where there is a chance to bag someone from out of state.

One ingredient in the delivery game that many forget is the interest of the federal government in the bigger cases. Even grass can get the attention of the DEA if the deal includes larger quantities and interstate transportation. And the federal sentencing guidelines (described in detail later) can make things ugly in a hurry for the local guy who gets tangled up with those who bring in several pounds of green for resale here. And to make things worse, people arrested in connection with drug delivery are often considered to be flight risks by the courts, so their bail bonds are set high enough that they typically cannot get out of jail pending trial. Again I say, drug involvement is a really stupid way to destroy one's life.

▶Plea Bargains in Drug Cases

While pleading to a charge where only minor possession is involved is pretty routine, those who face delivery counts can expect a very different kind of adventure. Experienced lawyers are again a must, because, unlike other felony cases, here the cops typically demand some kind of performance for a defendant to get a break. Again, this means "cooperation" with authorities, including information, setting up buys, wearing a wire, and even testifying. And although most public defenders are competent to work out such arrangements, having counsel who is well familiar with the individual cops and their usual practices in such cases is crucial. Knowledgeable and sophisticated defense counsel can help avoid some of the more dire consequences of such arrangements—sometimes. So aside from staying out of this sewer in the first place, the best advice is to keep one's mouth shut, get good counsel, and be prepared to take some risks. Attorney Dennis Zahn, an old friend and a guy I have always trusted with such difficult and complicated cases, once helped us guide a high school student through this kind of mine field, and the kid eventually avoided jail *and helped the cops* without facing too much danger. However, the boy's mother expressed a predictably different view of the whole affair.

In any event, be prepared to make a deal that gives the authorities something of value to them in their ongoing war with the drug trade, or be just as prepared to go to jail. Winning an acquittal in a possession or delivery case, especially where the delivery has been to an informant or undercover officer, is usually a pipe dream; again, best policy—stay away from recreational substances. Period.

DOMESTIC VIOLENCE

The problems attendant to this area are so complex that we would need a whole book just for the subject. The phrase "domestic violence" has taken on meaning in our society far beyond that which traditionally it had, which was limited to the marital relationship, as society has begun to recognize and even embrace all kinds of intimate, monogamous, residential arrangements that include some kind of at least temporary commitment between the parties. So the criminal law followed that route, constructing a special set of rules and a special kind of battery charge just for those who, while engaged in such a "relationship"—whether or not fleeting or unpredictable—inflict physical damage to each other. But what makes the area so complicated is the presence of several competing kinds of jurisdiction between various kinds of courts, including those with authority over divorce proceedings, various county and other courts that address the so-called "no contact" orders and other types of restraining orders, and forums with criminal jurisdiction.

The short version is that a battery committed against one's spouse, live-in cohabitant, or other like relation, is a Class A misdemeanor. The same offense, if committed in the same way, and with the same result, would be a Class B misdemeanor if the victim were *not* such class of person. The "domestic" label also extends to persons who are divorced from each other or who have previously lived together "as a spouse" of the accused, and to all persons who have borne a child together. And the whole thing turns into a Class D felony if the defendant has previously been convicted of striking the same person. So, as we will see in the section on sentencing, striking—*battering*—becomes a higher degree of misdemeanor when the object of the striking is such "related" person. And while it may seem an odd result, one should simply accept that this difference has been the result of lawmakers wrestling with a huge epidemic of battered wives, girlfriends, paramours, common law wives, and unwed mothers. Men have nobody to blame but themselves for this strange result.

What is important to understand here is that, in addition to facing charges for this unconsented to and unprivileged touching, posting bond, and hiring a lawyer, the defendant in such case can expect to be banned from his residence if the victim lives there, too, and can be guaranteed to be the target of an ironclad restraining order. And any breach of that order will be cause for revocation of bond and an extended stay in the local jail until the case is concluded.

▶ *Victims*

Victims need to have copies of the orders restraining the defendant in their possession at all times, and it makes sense to talk to the local police concerning how they will respond in the event of a violation of that order. Today it is common for the violator to go straight to jail, so long as the police have proof the person so restrained has come around the person to be protected by the order. However, this rule is not to be trusted. There are still police agencies that hesitate or even refuse to make such an arrest without additional violence occurring or at least some breach of the peace in connection with the violation of the order. It should not be so, but there are still instances where it is. Some police still take the "it's a civil matter" attitude, refusing to make an arrest where they see the case as merely enforcement of a civil order. So, if you have received an order protecting you from a significant other, check with police, sheriff, or marshal to be sure you know what they will do if Bozo shows up for a return engagement.

Restraining orders do not keep doors locked or stop the phone from ringing, and they are not bulletproof; you have a piece of paper that is as effective as the batterer's respect for the law that produced it. Anyone who has been the victim of domestic violence has to recognize that, as Yogi said, "it ain't over until it's over," and the issuance of a no-contact order is just the beginning of the solution, not the end. You must be your own best friend—and the best friend to the kids if there are any in this mess—and take every available step to protect yourself. That means keeping people around you, spending time with family and friends, and being vigilant. And one more thing: *keep your mouth shut and stay away from him!* While it is true that no one "asks for it" when it comes to being abused, it is sadly true that many people, themselves imperfect and wrapped up in emotional conflict, anger, and their own set of resentments, contribute to the situation by permitting or even encouraging contact. Nothing will infuriate a judge faster than having a victim of domestic violence who ends up back in harm's way *on purpose,* after having already suffered enough to know better, and after having insisted that the court intervene to protect her.

While it is true that folks can and sometimes do work things out, there is a right way to approach that challenge, and it does not include permitting or encouraging prohibited contact in violation of court order. The place to begin again is in the counselor's office, the pastor's study, or at some family resource center. We know for certain that repeat incidences of battery tend to become ever more violent and dangerous. In my twenty-five years of homicide work, it was rarely the case that one spouse killed the other the first time they got crossways. You can't help what has already happened, but for everyone's sake you have to do all you can to prevent it from happening again.

▶Defendants

It's a very thin sheet of paper that only has one side, and that old adage applies in spades to cases of domestic violence. That said, most of the time the charges are well founded, and if that is the case, the first and best thing to do is to admit it to yourself and take a crash course in growing up. The vast majority of defendants in these cases are the men, for obvious and undeniable reasons. And for reasons just as obvious, when they commit such acts, the results are typically more injurious than those committed by women. So there is understandably a lot more attention paid to what men do during the pendancy of cases that arise out of claims against them, and the courts tend to follow them with more interest after the cases have been concluded. And that holds true for those that are handled by the divorce court, the domestic violence courts, or a court with criminal jurisdiction. Moreover, the more serious the incident that leads to the charges being filed, the more attention the guy can expect after the fact. Here is some basic advice for anyone accused of domestic battery, stalking, intimidation, or violation of a court-issued no-contact order:

> 1. Stay away from the alleged victim. Period. No phone calls, no drive-bys, no letters or messages via third parties. It may be painful, especially when that means not having contact with your kids for a while, but that's what "no-contact" means—**no contact.** Separate arrangements for visiting with kids can be made through counsel or, if the order comes from a divorce or domestic violence court, can be made a part of the order that the court enters. In such cases, use grandparents, aunts and uncles, pastors,

or neutral friends as intermediaries for pick-up and delivery of the children, carefully avoiding forbidden contact with the ex. Beyond the obvious violation of the court's order, there is the specter of a repeat engagement in the violence department. When one of my clients in a divorce case got a restraining order against her husband, she thought she was safe, and he thought it was just a piece of paper. They were both wrong. He found her, beat her mercilessly, then went to jail for over two months. The divorce was eventually granted, her injuries healed, but he lost it all. He really never recovered from that stint in the Marion County Jail.

2. Take the initiative where counseling or other court-ordered activities are indicated. This means drug or alcohol programs if either of those are an issue in your case, as well as individual counseling to address whatever the underlying causes of the whole meltdown might have been. So called "anger control" counseling is often required in such cases, and even though there may have been extenuating circumstances that would explain much of what happened, such counseling will be ordered anyway. As the man says, "just do it." The very best way to avoid some of the more dire consequences of domestic violence prosecutions is to demonstrate to the court that you have done everything in your power to see that such behavior is never repeated. A judge who sees a well-groomed man who maintains a full time job, supports and cares for his kids, has quit drinking, done all the counseling, and otherwise been a model citizen, is likely to take all that into account.

3. Avoid bad company, and stay away from the places and the people that may have contributed to things falling apart and getting violent. If money played a role in the collapse of the relationship and ultimately led to the violence, usually there was somebody who was wasting it. If that somebody was you, stop it. Taverns, bowling alleys, nightclubs, poker games, and casinos are all just giant,

swirling drains that suck money away from those who go there. And remember—if you have been charged with domestic violence in the divorce context, all that misconduct will only encourage the judge to saddle you with more of the debt that flowed from such excesses. Avoiding such places and habits, such as booze, dope, and other recreational substances, will save huge cash, in addition to keeping you out of harm's way. The guy who gets busted for fighting in some gin mill after already being charged with domestic violence can expect to get the undivided and severely unfriendly attention of the judge.

4. If you want to repair the now injured or broken relationship, you can't fix it directly, as the court will toss you in jail if you attempt to communicate with your estranged significant other. That's where the lawyer can be of assistance. He can talk to opposing counsel, or to the prosecutor in the criminal setting, and they can talk about the idea of joint counseling, even asking the court to amend the existing order to provide for such contact. Another husband whose wife was my client got treated to a visit from the sheriff when the case was filed. They took him to his house, waited while he got his toothbrush and some clean undies, and then explained that he would be jailed if he showed up again. It must have been a serious gut-check moment, because his lawyer convinced us he was a changed man (after twenty years of beating his wife) and they got back together with resounding and apparently permanent success. But of course, all this presupposes that the alleged batterer behaves with priest-like purity in the interim.

The modern family has been so decimated by the huge changes in American culture over the past thirty years that it appears to be a truly endangered species. There can be no doubt that the incidence of violence within the family has exploded over that time, for which there have been many causes. Of course, having begun to embrace all manner of heretofore-unacceptable behavior as "family" or even just "relationship," society got all the trappings and unfixable flaws that attend such nonsense. The old saying is still true, that there are no atheists in foxholes, and certainly persons facing the kind of hell that is implicated in any domestic violence case must recognize that they are indeed in an awful war, with a big piece of the battle their own fault. So be it politically incorrect and socially unacceptable—pray about it. Alone or together, pray for mending the fence or just allowing wounds to heal in a new life; that's the only prescription I know of that is guaranteed to work.

FELONIES

For those involved in a criminal prosecution, whether as victim, defendant, witness, or family member of one of those, or even at times those who work in the case, there is a huge difference between felony cases and the lesser crimes. Worse things have been done, more harm has been suffered, and the sentences are by definition longer. A felony, by long-standing usage in Indiana, was any crime for which one may be incarcerated in a penitentiary. This did not include the county jail or a juvenile detention center, but meant everything else. Now that ends up also typically meaning that the sentence will be for more than a year, as the jails won't usually keep an inmate longer than that. Felonies are divided into classes, D through A, with A being the most serious. Here is the list:

1. Class D felonies include most of the theft charges, marijuana possession or delivery where the quantity is over thirty (30) grams, second offense drunk-driving convictions or others where there is injury associated with the case, second offense firearms violations (no license, etc.), battery convictions where there is bodily injury or assault on a police officer, child exploitation, and some sex offenses. There are many more, but these make up the basic skeleton. The sentences then are set as "determinate" terms, with the presumptive sentence being a year and one-half, to which can be added another year and one-half, or from which

can be subtracted one year, depending on the circumstances. All or any portion of that sentence can be suspended by the court in most cases.

2. Class C felonies include bigger drug charges, forgery and several of the other check or negotiable instrument crimes, reckless homicide, aggravated assault cases (more serious injuries) and some of the more serious sex crimes. That range of sentences includes a presumptive sentence of four years of incarceration, to which can be added another four, or from which can be taken two. So the range is from two to eight years. Sentences are suspendable, and many of these crimes get that kind of treatment, especially where serious injury is missing or there is no prior record of serious misconduct.

3. Class B felonies are much more serious, including the big time crimes like robbery, kidnapping, rape, arson, and residence burglary, where in each case there is no serious physical injury to the victim. That sentence is a presumptive ten-year confinement, to which can be added as much as ten more, or from which as much as four years can be deducted. Most of these are suspendable as well, although commission of any of these with a deadly weapon can make those crimes nonsuspendable.

4. Class A crimes are the most serious of all, with only murder carrying stiffer penalties. These include all the felonies under the Class B list, where those also include infliction of serious bodily injury to the victim. In addition attempted murder and conspiracy to commit murder are also A's. The penalty is a presumptive determinative sentence of thirty years, to which can be added twenty years for aggravating circumstances, and from which can be subtracted ten years for mitigation. The whole aggravating/mitigation thing is really too complicated for us here, but basically what the law does is to recognize that sometimes crimes are committed in such a way as to make them worse than others. How serious the injuries are to

those hurt by the defendant, the length and content of the defendant's criminal record, and the absence of any remorse for the behavior can all cause the court to consider adding years to the presumptive sentence. Conversely, the youthfulness of the offender, the fact that his or her role in the crime was relatively minor, assistance provided to law enforcement during investigation and arrest of other suspects, and pleading guilty and expressing remorse for the crimes all will help get the court to consider lessening the sentence.

5. Murder is, in every way, in a class by itself. The sentences for murder include a presumptive forty-year period of incarceration, to which can be added twenty, and from which can be subtracted as much as ten years. The death penalty will apply where the killing is intentional and was committed while the defendant was involved in committing one of several violent crimes, like robbery, arson, rape, kidnapping, burglary, and the like. In addition, intentional killing of a police or corrections officer, judge, prosecutor, or firefighter is a capital offense. The procedure is a bit complex for trying a death penalty case, as it includes special rules for impaneling the jury, and often includes keeping the jury together throughout the case (sequestration), and a separate additional hearing before the jury after conviction to determine whether or not the death penalty is appropriate. The jury's role is that of advisor only here, as they make a recommendation to the court. The court is then solely responsible for the final decision. I have been involved in the prosecution of a dozen capital cases, and they are no picnic. Of those, I actually tried five, and three of those ended in an execution. All three were horrible crimes, two involving the murder of police officers and one of an innocent, hard-working cab driver. I am truly sorry those executions had to occur, but with the perspective of time on my side now, I can tell you that their punishment fit the crime and was richly deserved in every instance.

All the classes also include the potential for fines, up to $10,000 for Class D and C felonies, and up from there for B's and A's. That seldom matters in these cases, as the defendants have no money and are sent into confinement for long enough not to be able to earn the money anyway.

Sentencing

All sentencing in Indiana is done by the court, without input from any jury except for death cases. There the jury makes only a recommendation, and that is not binding on the court. However, expect there to be consistency for similar crimes. First-time offenders whose crimes do not include injury or loss of life typically do not go to prison, or at least they do not go for long. However, the big ingredient here is prior record, as well as conduct after the present charges were brought. Those with a bad history, and specifically those who get into more trouble while the case is pending, can expect to go away for a while. Even Mike Tyson, a first-time offender, got the same executed prison sentence that Judge Gifford had given to others who were not so famous but had committed rape as a Class B felony.

Again, it is crucial that the criminal defendant has competent counsel, someone who knows the prosecutor's guidelines and who also knows how the courts in that county handle sentencing. Whether or not the lawyer provided as a public defender is effective depends on the county, although we have come to associate a high degree of professionalism with these public defenders in most places. Certainly they are very competent in the larger metropolitan areas, and my own experience with them in smaller communities has been good as well.

It is so important to recognize that every felony charge is serious. A record for almost any Class D felony will probably blacklist the offender from holding any job that requires a security clearance, the handling of other people's money, or requires the person applying to be capable of being bonded. No one with a felony conviction can work in law enforcement, carry a gun, or work in a bank.

There are a few exceptions to all that, but the best result is always to avoid the felony conviction at all. Whether it's writing bad checks or holding up liquor stores, felonies are not trivial, so get a good lawyer and cooperate with that lawyer completely.

FEDERAL COURT

A whole 'nuther smoke, to be sure. The federal system is complex, rigid, and unfriendly. The crimes for which people get prosecuted by the feds tend to be bigger and have higher dollar losses associated with them, and the quality of investigation is typically very high. But the biggest mystery to those who end up in federal custody is the federal sentencing guidelines. These are a draconian matrix of arbitrary and at times brutal categories and options used by the judges to determine every sentence—and there are few options. If a judge attempts to exercise any real discretion or to recognize any of the human circumstances that he or she might feel are worthy of consideration *outside those guidelines,* the U.S. Attorney will appeal the sentence, and the appellate courts quickly reverse it.

As is obvious, I don't like them. They strip our judges of the authority to be judges; we claim to pick the best of the bunch to hold these lifetime appointments, then handcuff them, telling them they are incompetent to follow the statute and mete out punishment in a moral and appropriate way. But that's the game, so get ready. Whatever the guideline matrix yields, that's what you get. Period. One who finds himself the target of a federal investigation is well advised to make quick tracks to the lawyer's office, and that lawyer needs to be in touch with authorities at once, learning whether or not early disposition can occur, before the federal grand jury returns an indictment.

CHAPTER FOUR
⚖ Employment Relations

T̲O WORK IS TO EXPERIENCE LIFE AT ITS MOST BASIC—AND AT TIMES, AT ITS most complex. The fundamental equation is pretty simple: you work, they pay you money. The rest is fluff. At least that's the way things have been historically in Indiana. The advent of the whole array of anti-discrimination laws, equal pay legislation, special rules for people with disabilities (however loosely defined) not to mention collective bargaining law and agreements, have made for an interesting and often unknowable body of law.

Indiana has been—and with few exceptions remains today—an "at will" state. That is to say, the employer hires the employee "at will," to work at the will of the employer, and when the employer or the employee wants out, the music stops. In Indiana a person can be terminated from his or her job with or without cause, for lots of reasons or for no reason at all. The boss can be a jerk, favor one employee over another, treat everyone like dirt, fire on Monday and re-hire the next morning a thousand times if he likes, and the employee basically has no recourse. What we will address here are the few areas where there is any real departure from this simple concept.

EMPLOYMENT DISCRIMINATION

There was a time when the easiest case a lawyer could take to federal court was one that claimed the client had been discriminated against in violation of Title VII of the 1964 Civil Rights Act. Race, creed, color, national origin, or gender were the so-called "protected classifications," discreet and identifiable populations of people whose common physical, ethnic, or national characteristics gave them protection under that law. My first reasonably nice fee as a lawyer came as plaintiff's counsel for a woman who had been passed over for promotion in a mail-order clothing company after declining the district manager's proposals for a bit of extracurricular nightlife. In those days, to plead was to win, as the whole world seemed fixated on the concept of legislated fairness and statutorily mandated "being nice." But as the old men say, "them days're gone."

The basic idea of both the federal and our state laws on discrimination was simple. While we couldn't make everyone be nice to his or her neighbors, we could legislate some measure of bias- or harassment-free environment in the workplace. So, for those whose employers had a sufficient number of employees (the old number was fifteen) it became unlawful to discriminate in employment practices, based on those criteria. For hiring, retention, promotion, benefit qualification, tenure, advancement, and training, as well as a whole list of retirement-related subjects, an employer who favored one color over another, one nationality over another, or one gender over another found there were penalties and damages that would flow from such misconduct. These statutes all still apply today. Until you file suit, that is.

Today, except for race, much of the original vitality and authority of the law has been eroded by a long and ever-more unfriendly string of court decisions relating mostly to the area of gender discrimination. Of course it was the excess of the early glory days of sex discrimination litigation that was to blame for this more recent animosity toward those cases in our federal courts, owing largely to that era that once made it a violation of the law even to compliment a lady on her new dress. We can all remember those ridiculous cases, borne of the radical feminist delusional views of men as the great social and societal evil, dirty boys with one-track minds. Well, from that truly hideous perversion of the law, we got an onslaught of cases in the federal system that over time resulted in some 70% of all cases filed there being Title VII related. Now the opposite extreme has become reality, and men can run roughshod over their female counterparts and subordinates, groping, disrespecting, and even driving them away altogether. And the judges on the courts of appeal steadily issue rafts of opinions sustaining the dismissal of those claims, declaring in the face of some really awful male misconduct that "Title VII was never intended to be a civility code." Maybe not, Judge, but it sure was intended to be more than it is now. Here is a brief overview of the various protected classifications.

▶*Gender*

This was always the big one, but no more. If a woman can prove that the males with whom she works have so discriminated against her *because of her gender*, that she is essentially physically precluded from doing her job, and further that such conduct has produced a working environment so hostile that it affects the "conditions of her employment," she may have a claim. This of course presupposes that she has made timely complaint, and that the employer has failed to take appropriate, prompt, effective remedial action—whatever that is. Sounds like a trick bag? That's precisely what it is. Said another way, the glory days of sex discrimination litigation for plaintiffs are gone. And what has happened—in large measure due to the pure exasperation of federal judges with the sheer numbers of cases clogging their dockets—is that things can be about as bad for women in the workplace now as they were before the statute took effect.

Make no mistake, it is not a level playing field between men and women in the market these days, and that holds true as much in the blue collar and union environment as it does inside the carpeted offices of corporate America. So why bother with complaining at all? Because it will only be through tenacious perseverance by women and their lawyers that some of these injustices will be remedied. If you know you're being harassed, propositioned, ignored, passed over, or left with the trash work while the boys continue to skim the gravy, there can be no choice but to make a stand—and a complaint. The only real strength in this area lies in claims of retaliation, where the woman is in some way punished for having complained of such misconduct. With such a claim and adequate proof that it happened in retaliation for complaints made, even today's unfriendly federal forums relent and rule for the woman. We'll address later the Equal Employment Opportunity Commission (EEOC) and making timely claims there, but for now, be clear that you have only a total of three hundred days after the last act of discrimination in which to act. And going to the EEOC at all is a waste of time unless you have first taken up your grievances with the appropriate people in your company's employ, who are responsible for investigating them. If you keep good records, document the evidence that supports your claim, and act in a timely manner, it's worth it to raise the issues. We have handled half a dozen harassment cases in the past year, and with the mediation process helping, have had pretty good results for women. But make no mistake, it's not a fair fight. And the challenges are not all in the courtroom. One of my clients saw her case collapse last year when the men in the union local, who were to testify for her, developed amnesia—each and every one of them. All I'll say about men in those organizations is that it appears they collectively have forgotten all their mothers ever tried to teach them about manners and respect. We will not go further into the many confusing elements and conflicts in the current case law, so just be aware that you face a tough task if the basis of your claim of discrimination is gender.

▶*Race*

Certainly our society has made huge strides in alleviating this form of discrimination, but vestiges of it still remain in some places. To make a case for race discrimination, more is necessary than mere use of racially unfriendly rhetoric or the appearance of some impolite behavior by co-workers or supervisory personnel. As has been the case in gender cases, the courts have become more stringent in their requirements for proof of discriminatory behavior, and there must be some connection between the complaint of conduct and losses suffered by the complainant. One can expect somewhat better reception than that awaiting the gender claim from both the EEOC and the courts, but the days are gone when simply alleging that racial slur has occurred will be enough to spell victory. What still resonates well with the courts is the claim that demonstrates that hiring, promotion, benefits, or seniority rules are either skewed against one race or are applied in such a way as to achieve a discriminatory result. If one expects to prevail in a race case now, it is necessary to produce affirmative proof of such a claim; mere subjective conclusions by the complaining party that race is somehow involved won't cut it.

▶National origin; religion

These cases are more rare, although we have had them. Often these are based upon some built-in animosity toward those from other countries, typically centering on appearance, speech, dress, or perceived difference in job performance. The key here is connecting the behavior with the ethnicity of the complainant. "I just can't stand those Germans" or "ain't that just like a Jew?!" are the kind of epithets that make it easy to get things rolling for the lawyer, but even such invective will be insufficient unless you can provide proof that those expressed attitudes led to some kind of demonstrably discriminatory effect *in the workplace*. Without that, all the boorish talk in the world is unlikely to persuade a judge to award damages. Moreover, there is little chance the EEOC will spend much time on it either. Our recent experience in this regard has been with foreign professional people, and the intense animosity demonstrated by management toward them has been astonishing to behold. One woman healthcare professional drew every night and weekend assignment in the place for over a year, and when she asked that things be balanced out, the physician who was responsible for her scheduling first acknowledged the facts, then promptly declared that he didn't care.

▶Age

If you're over forty and get fired or replaced, you have an age discrimination claim, right? Wrong. But if you're over forty, have done good work, cost more than a younger person in the same job would cost, and get replaced by a kid who is "twenty-something," the possibilities begin to appear. The short version of a very knotty area is that getting replaced by younger personnel because they are cheaper, either from the salary perspective or based upon the cost of benefits to the older folk, ain't kosher. The problem from the employer's perspective is that such economic considerations can become so significant that companies go to all kind of lengths to accomplish the voluntary replacement of older with younger. One major corporation employing hundreds (at least) in Indiana crafted a deal they called the "bridge to retirement," an incentive plan intended to interest the over-forty crowd in leaving in favor of younger, cheaper people. The rub always came when the older employee, happy in the job, making good money, and with no interest in going somewhere else, declined. At times, such plans have ended up becoming characterized by some pretty heavy-handed tactics intended to convince the unwilling older worker to take the tendered deal. In one of our cases, the employee expressed no interest, and then to no one's surprise, her annual evaluations began to nose-dive. Others found themselves the unhappy recipients of notices that their jobs had been "restructured" out of existence, making the early-out option much more appealing. Of course litigation ensued when the nice people in personnel also informed our client that, because of the restructuring and our client's failure to take the deal previously offered, the offer was no longer available. The rule is pretty simple: one cannot be discriminated against with regard to hiring, retention, advancement, compensation, or benefits qualifications based upon age. The operative age limit is forty, so if you get the golden shaft after that age, it's worth consulting counsel and visiting the EEOC to discuss the likelihood of a claim.

The essential point here is that these cases no longer carry the weight and authority they once did. I think most plaintiff's lawyers in this area would agree that racial cases are still the strongest, and even those are more difficult to win than they were twenty years ago. Much of that is due to some real changes in the workplace, and those changes have thankfully made some of the more hateful conduct uncommon. And it is also good that simply making such an accusation is no longer instantly accepted as true, thereby creating an immediate presumption of guilt against the person alleged to have committed the discriminatory acts. One who would allege that his or her failure to accomplish the kind of advancement, pay increase, or bonus that the employee felt should occur must at least respond to the employer's claimed defense that points out performance or other job-related criteria as the reason for the disparity between the complainant's treatment and that accorded others. The worker's complaint that the white guys are getting more raises and quicker advancement up the bureaucratic food chain is quickly blunted when job performance differences are documented and clear. One whose attendance, training session grades, disciplinary record, or success in learning new or changed procedures or tasks can be shown to have been poor can no longer hide behind ethnicity as the "real reason" for his failure to move up the ladder. Moreover, as we will address in the employer's section below, the presence of affirmative policies and procedures put in place by the boss to avoid discrimination have gone a long way in reducing the number of incidences of real misconduct that occur.

THE EMPLOYER'S PERSPECTIVE

The law requires that employers have in place a procedure for workers to follow when they experience—or *believe they have experienced*—prohibited discrimination in the workplace. Obviously no judge is going to be very impressed with such a procedure that requires the employee to make the complaint to the person whom they believe is responsible for the problem, so there must be someone up the ladder or outside the chain of command to whom complaints can be made. The logic here is that no one can guarantee a discrimination-free environment, but once it happens there must be a mechanism in place to address it in a prompt and effective way. So test your response plan against this measure. Is your action prompt? Effective? Aimed at remedying the problem? Responsive to the problem presented? If so, and if you actually follow that policy in practice, the chances of a court finding against you are slim. Of course, that action must actually *work* when taken, and if it does not, then the offending employee will have to be disciplined, moved, or terminated in order for your actions to have been deemed appropriate and sufficient.

There are hundreds, even thousands, of publications that treat the many issues and problems that attend this area from the employer's side, so we won't attempt to outwit those who provide such advice. But the real point is that everyone who employs people *must* pay attention to these difficult issues. Failure to do so will almost certainly subject that employer to either state or federal sanctions, including fines, penalties, damages, and attorney's fees when the inevitable discrimination charge occurs. Employers can't really keep claims from being made, but they can have a huge impact on whether or not the claims are successful, and that all depends on the policies—and the implementation of them—mentioned above.

There is, however, a real reason for paying serious attention to these matters, whether or not they ever lead to legal action. Women, minorities, and older workers are so much a part of the workplace, and their contributions are so important, that any environment that puts their well-being in jeopardy is almost certain to impact the efficiency and productivity of the company. Those who recognize that the old "glass ceiling" is still alive and well, especially for women, and who take steps to fix it in their businesses, are only exercising sound professional judgment. Besides, passing the women over in favor of the guys, or refusing to recognize that one of the boys is being an insufferable jerk to every woman in the office, or permitting a guy to patronize or even mistreat minority personnel, is more than bad form—it's just plain wrong.

Just last year, a high level, high profile male superstar, responsible for an operation of international significance, finally caught his lunch thanks to our brave woman client. The guy had insulted and denigrated every woman in sight from the first day he was on the job, and management repeatedly ignored his continued pattern of misconduct. And in addition to his sexual transgressions, he possessed a huge temper and an extremely vulgar tongue when angered. His people were terrified of him, and he made it clear to one and all that complaints about him would result in a fate worse than death—intense punishment and eventual termination. It took some pretty strong proof to awaken sleeping management, but the boss finally got a bellyful of listening to the complaints and fired the guy. They also paid reasonable damages to our client, as well.

It is my prediction that, unless those in positions of authority begin taking steps to fix some of the deeply held attitudes that still infect the men in high places, new and much more punitive legislation will come along to make things more difficult than they already are. We have made great strides in the area of race and age discrimination, but evidence of a huge and pervasive bias against the promotion and compensation of women, *based solely on gender,* is overwhelming. And the recent high-speed retreat by the federal courts from sanctioning such misconduct has in large measure frustrated the specific intent of the statute.

WAGE CLAIMS

There is a simple rule for the payment of wages and other regular compensation in Indiana: Pay or get sued. The statute requires that compensation such as wages, overtime, commissions, and unpaid vacation time be paid to the departing employee within fifteen days of the last day the employee was employed. After that date, the unpaid amounts bear interest at the whopping rate of 10% **per day** up to double the amount owed, plus reasonable attorney's fees. That ends up amounting to *triple damages.* Very few employers know about this provision, but it has huge teeth, and the cost of refusing to pay timely can be really painful. For example, when a real estate salesperson leaves the employ of an agency and has $2,500 in commissions due but unpaid, after about twenty-five days from date of departure for the agent the amount owed turns into a neat $7,500, and if suit is required, the agency pays the lawyer, too. Easily a ten grand mistake. There are some nuances concerning some of these calculations, but this is pretty close, so employers beware! It's expensive to hold up former employees. Interestingly, this rule is truly ancient in its origin, coming right straight out of the Good Book, Deuteronomy 24:15. Guess that might make it carry just a bit more weight, huh?

CHAPTER FIVE
⚖ **Real Estate**

IT'S THE MOST UNIQUE POSSESSION A PERSON CAN ACQUIRE. OVER TIME ITS uses are almost limitless, and as the man says, "they're not making any more of it." Ground is one of the surest and safest ways to accumulate and keep wealth because it can be expected to hold its value, and each new use that comes along typically increases it. So understanding the basics of the law surrounding this precious commodity is very important, and knowing the difference between myth and fable and the truth where real estate law is concerned is key.

PRINCIPLES OF BUYING/SELLING PROPERTY

One of the most often-litigated problems in most states is the actual, basic rule about the transfer of property and the requirements for entering into binding contracts for its transfer. Let's quickly get two powerfully important rules straight, then we can address how they work and some limited exceptions to them. First, **the only way to transfer title to real estate is by deed.** Promises do not accomplish transfer and neither do contracts, and once a deed is executed and tendered to the transferee, it is conclusive. That act can only be undone by another deed that transfers it back to the transferor or by a court order that "sets the deed aside," thereby nullifying it. So *if you don't have a deed, you don't have title.* Secondly, **all contracts agreeing to transfer real estate must be in writing.** A promise to deed property, an unsigned contract or other document containing a promise to do so, or even a repeated custom or practice to sell without a written promise are ineffective to bind a person to such a promise unless there is writing "signed by the party to be charged."

As to deeds, there is more to this than meets the untrained eye. Folks who try to accomplish real estate sales and other transfers without proper advice often end up spending thousands of dollars on years of litigation for having failed to get the deed right. A defective deed, in the typical case, is simply ineffective to transfer title at all. So Joe sells Sam his house, writes up the deed himself, and gets part of the legal description to the property wrong. Ten years later, when Sam tries to sell to Pete, Pete has a title search done by a title insurance company, discovering the error. The result? Sam has defective title, must file suit to attempt a fix for the error, and Pete goes on to buy some other property. The deed created a false title in property that was never owned by Joe or Sam, so the folks who own the incorrectly-included property get drawn in, resulting in a heated courtroom situation. Although a worst case scenario, you can see the kind of disaster possibly flowing from having failed to have a deed properly drawn and executed.

One more thing: in Indiana, we are what's called a "notice state" because the first guy to record his deed wins. So where Sam deeds property to Joe, but then decides he's got a better offer from Pete, if Pete records his deed at the recorder's office before Joe gets there (so long as Pete was innocent of wrongdoing or knowledge of the claims of Sam) the ground belongs to Pete. So the rule is that only a deed delivered to the transferee transfers title, but it is also essential to protect that transaction by recording that deed at once.

With regard to contracts, in almost every jurisdiction in the United States, there is a thing called the Statute of Frauds. This set of rules find its roots in England several hundred years ago, and the ancient version of it dealt with a number of "frauds" to be avoided by requiring a written agreement to make certain transactions effective. There were several things addressed, but for our purposes, the rule stated that no contract for the sale of real estate could be effective unless the contract was in writing, and had been signed by the party "to be charged," a phrase that meant the party against whom enforcement was being attempted. So where the seller promises to sell the property, but there is no writing that bears his signature, the basic rule is that that seller cannot be required to make good on the promise. If the promise is in writing, Indiana provides for "specific performance" against the seller, so that the buyer can force the seller to deliver a deed and thereby sell to him. Not so the other way around. If a buyer who has signed an agreement to purchase property backs out, the court will not force him to buy, but instead the court can award damages to the seller if he ends up losing money on the deal. The point: **GET IT IN WRITING AND MAKE SURE THE OTHER SIDE SIGNS THE AGREEMENT.**

Here is a short list of important considerations when buying or selling:

1. Get it in writing.

2. Brokers aren't lawyers. The good ones know it and don't attempt to give legal advice (at least not very often) but real estate people are sales people first, and advice on the law from them is probably right *most of the time.* But the small stuff gets past 'em too often, and they are notoriously poor drafters of documents where the details can be dangerous.

3. When buying, insist on an inspection by someone who is licensed and bonded to perform such services. Also read carefully the forms now required of sellers in residential transactions. If the inspection report tells a different story than the sellers' disclosures, there is reason to be mistrustful. When selling, be careful about that form, and get it right. If you've had leaks, breaks, water, HV/AC problems, termites, or any other real problem, disclose it. Failure to do so is actionable and may constitute fraud. There is now a statute that covers this area, and you are required to comply with its terms. See I.C. 24-4-4.6-1. This is the citation to the Indiana statute that now governs these transactions.

4. If you are buying/selling without a broker, check out the details with legal counsel and be sure the lawyer reviews the contract, the proposed deed, and any other documents you produce. This includes the results of the title search done by the title insurance company, which must

be reviewed carefully. And this means always—ALWAYS—requiring and providing title insurance.

5. If you are buying, it is your sole responsibility to see that the deed you receive is correct and that it is properly recorded after being executed and delivered to you. This means checking the legal description against that contained in the title policy "binder"—the preliminary paperwork provided by the title insurance company before closing—and taking the original deed to the recorder's office to be properly entered into its system of records. The deed must be notarized, and it must contain a recitation that tells who prepared it. The County Recorder will take the document, record it, and make notations on the original that show the recording has been done, then return the original to the place you designate. The whole process may take several months in the larger counties, so it may be necessary to check on the status of the original deed if it fails to get returned. The actual recording happens at once, but getting it back with all the new notations often takes time. Ask the folks at the recorder's office at the time you record the instrument how long you should expect to wait for its return.

ENCUMBRANCES

This ancient word means little to most people, but in some way it enters into virtually every real estate transaction. In general, the term "encumbrance" means any limitation on the ownership, use, or right to transfer property, where that limitation is passed on to whomever you sell or transfer to. So mortgages, driveway or fence line easements, local or subdivision covenants restricting use, mechanics' liens, and in some ways even zoning ordinances, all are encumbrances. The reason I mention them at all is that each of these (and a zillion more I did not list) impacts the right to hold, use, transfer, and change the land you buy. The mortgage your predecessor gave his father-in-law to secure his loan, the claim of the driveway contractor for installation your predecessor never paid for, and the minimum square footage, lot size, type of construction, and minimum setback from boundary lines are all limitations on your ownership and use, and each will pass on to the next owner, thereby "running with the land" unless you take the right steps to remove them.

Things like restrictive covenants that appear on the face of the deed are of huge significance here, and one horror story will serve to show just how important it can be to read these things before accepting them. Clients of ours agreed with their seller *before they bought the property* that they would be permitted to add an outbuilding for purposes of housing my client's tools and equipment. The parties even talked about providing an additional access to the place from an alternative direction. Well the guy not only "forgot" his promise, he inserted into the deed an express limitation that forbade the addition of *any improvements or structures* beyond the house to be built on the parcel. And because the sale was closed, not when the house was done, but when the mortgage company agreed to finance the construction, my clients paid little attention to the deed when they closed on the construction loan. Years later they decided to build the storage building, started construction, then got sued by their friendly neighbor, the widow of the now-deceased seller. She claimed that none of the promises made by her husband were actually made and demanded the building come down. This huge mess was made worse by the predictably obnoxious attitude and evil disposition of the widow, and in the end my clients had to capitulate with several nasty and most unfair demands by her because there simply was no way around this restrictive covenant that the deceased slickster had sneaked into the deed.

The zoning, subdivision restrictions, setbacks, and the like simply cannot be removed, as they define the nature of that type of development into which you have moved. Nobody gets to start raising sheep in his backyard in the Babbling Brook subdivision. No log cabins, racetracks, kennels, oil wells, high rise buildings, service stations, or junkyards are permitted, as the covenants in the documents that created the subdivision in the first place will not allow it.

Other things, like mortgages, mechanic's liens, unpaid taxes, or judgments, can and probably will have to be removed before you can buy or sell. Again, title insurance enters in, as the company will do a title search to discover any such claims, and in almost every case, the company will not insure the title unless those claims are cleared before the property is transferred. The important thing to remember with regard to these is that, although each identifies a claim for money against a person, it also impresses a lien against the property owned by that person at the time the debt was incurred, and that lien survives transfer. So, unless you get the old tax bill cleared up or the driveway contractor's lien paid and released, you will take title to the property subject to that claim, *and that claim will be superior to your own right of ownership.*

The rule again is the same: hire counsel when one of these problems arises, and don't wait until the closing date to do it. Sometimes these things can take time to fix, especially where they have existed for long periods before being discovered.

One particularly important type of cloud on the title to real estate is the mechanic's lien. A mechanic is anyone who works on the property and adds to it by his work. This can include maintenance and repair in addition to just building or adding things on. When a contractor or workman does work, the statute permits him to record a notice of his intention to hold a lien on the property if he does not get paid within sixty days of the last date on which he did work. The lien is good for one year, so you have to file suit to foreclose the lien within that time. However, where the work is done on property where a contractor has hired a subcontractor to do the work, notice of the unpaid balance and intention to hold the lien must be given to the actual owner before the lien can be recorded. Unless that has been done, the lien is ineffective against the owner of the property. Claiming and recording a mechanic's lien that is in error can result in liability against the mechanic, and the owner in such case may have what is called a "slander of title" action against him. My partner, Mike Kiefer, has done all this work for us for almost thirty years now, and many times we have seen those who are rightfully owed money for work performed miss out because they failed to act quickly enough or messed up the content and notices required by the law.

One of the most important features to the mechanic's lien is the presence of an attorneys' fee provision in the statute. It permits the mechanic to recover reasonable fees incurred in the collection of the amount owed but unpaid, so it is a pretty powerful weapon in the whole business of getting one's invoices collected. The home-owner who receives notice of the intention of a firm that has done work on the place to hold such a lien is well advised to make quick work of settling things on an amicable basis. Mike has been involved in the prosecution and defense of such cases scores of times, and the fact that the contractor can collect fees on top of what is owed for the work done can make losing an expensive proposition. On one occasion, the contractor claimed thousands of dollars in un-paid invoices for work done on the house, but Mike's client main-tained that the work had been poorly done and had cost thousands to get fixed. The problem from our client's perspective was that if the court didn't agree with the assessment of the poor workman-ship, our client would get stuck with all those bills *and a big attorneys' fee as well.* Eventually the case was settled, but the presence of those liens made things messy.

LANDLORDS VS. TENANTS

Both statutes and case law address this huge area of the law in Indiana, so we will provide an outline of the issues while not wear-ing you out with the many facets of the whole relationship. At some point in our lives, almost all of us end up renting a place to live or work. And while the lease you signed with Uncle Fred to rent his garage for your band to practice in may have been simple, those executed with the apartment complex for your first love nest or the one prescribed by the strip mall for your business are complicated, one-sided, long, and confusing. In the case of the commercial lease, there is little if any legislative protection, but there is a statute that governs residential leases.

The Indiana Landlord Tenant law is very specific concerning what a landlord can do when he or she has a beef with the tenant. Of course, one who fails to pay rent or keep the place up runs afoul of the provisions of most standard leases, and one need only repair to the local small claims or county court to get the offending folks out of the property. However, there are rights accorded tenants by the statute that cannot be waived by any lease provision, and efforts to lock out tenants, interrupt their utilities, or otherwise "interfere with" their rights of peaceful possession are unlawful and can give rise to damages. Doing so will result in such counterclaims, and the last thing a landlord can afford is a suit for damages filed by a mad tenant who is now represented by counsel, the Legal Aid Society, or a Legal Services Organization lawyer. Specifically, landlords must avoid the following:

> 1. Provisions in the lease that attempt to cause waiver of any statutory right; these include attempted waivers of the right to service of process and notice of any hearing for possession or damages, waiver of rights to possession in certain circumstances of default, or forfeiture of rights to possession of personal property.

> 2. Actions taken by the landlord to get into the premises in violation of the tenant's right to possession. Now this does not prohibit the landlord exercising his right of periodic inspection, as that is specifically protected by the law, but it denies "unreasonable access" that might be viewed as harassment.

> 3. Attempting to claim the right to hold the personal property of the tenant upon termination of the lease. You can get a security interest in property of the tenant by the tenant's execution of a *separate* document that pledges the property in the appropriate way, accompanied by a Uniform Commercial Code financing statement, the well-known "UCC-1" available at most stationers' stores. This gets filed with the Secretary of State in Indy and also can be recorded in the county recorder's office to perfect the landlord's claim in the property listed. But language in the lease that purports to either pledge the property of the tenant or provide for forfeiture of their stuff in the event of a default or abandonment of the premises is void.

> 4. Interrupting, terminating, or in any way withholding the utilities to the premises. This probably includes even

cable television service, but most certainly applies to water, sewer, gas, electricity, and telephone services. The local board of health can also be of great assistance here if the landlord has left the tenant in a condition that threatens the public health or safety. Tenants should not fail to make complaint or inquiry to those authorities as well if the situation warrants.

5. Failing to return all security deposits to the tenant minus deductions for lease violations and unpaid rent or utilities within forty-five days of the termination of the lease. This is a big one, and one for which we can thank the big landlords. The money has to go back within forty-five days of termination, accompanied by a written explanation of the reasons for all deductions and calculations to support them, unless the tenant fails to provide a forwarding address. The landlord cannot use the security deposit for repairs to the unit that are simply the result of ordinary wear and tear. So the rule is that replacing worn-out carpet, routine repainting of units, changing old appliances for new ones, new locks, and the like are *not* the tenant's problem. **A tenant whose security deposit is not returned in a timely fashion, and who has provided an address for its return, can sue for the money plus attorneys' fees.**

6. If the landlord sells his interest in the building that includes rental units, the landlord is relieved of liability for events happening after the date of notice of the transfer to the tenant. However, the landlord remains liable for any unreturned security deposits for a year after the transfer unless the purchaser of the building agrees to be liable. The tenant gets notice of the change and the selling landlord transfers the deposits to the purchasing landlord. *Seek counsel on this area and, if selling a rental place with tenants occupying at the time of sale, take strict precautions to protect their interests.*

7. Holding property of a tenant after termination of the

lease. A court can order removal of the tenant's stuff, and the landlord must then hire a warehouseman to hold it, subject to the court's order and the tenant's right to take possession of certain portions, whether the tenant pays for the storage or not. Things like medicine, medical appliances, "a week's supply of seasonably necessary clothing," and things needed to care for kids and their schooling, and blankets, must be turned over to the tenant by the storage people *without payment* when demand is made. The tenant remains liable for the storage cost of these items, but the warehouseman or landlord cannot condition delivery of them upon payment of that charge. The storage place can then sell the "nonexempt" property to pay the storage costs after ninety days. The statute gives us no wisdom on what is to happen to "exempt" property that goes unclaimed, but one would think a tenant would make some effort to get that back—maybe. In any event, if things this technical and sticky come up, call your lawyer.

Landlords can and often do represent themselves in small claims actions for possession of property and damages, with no ill effect. It is my advice that in any case where there is a known dispute between the parties before an action is filed, the landlord get legal advice before proceeding.

Tenants are obviously at risk in these cases, as the law still favors the landlord and his right to possess his property in the event of default or damage. One who believes his or her apartment or other dwelling agreement has been breached should have the problem checked out with counsel before doing anything rash. Withholding rent, making repairs and setting off the cost against rent, abandoning the place without notice, or just getting mad and messing things up are all bad ideas. A tenant with a beef should do these things:

1. Make timely and repeated complaint to the landlord or manager, and do it *in writing every time*. Keep copies of all that correspondence, as well as the responses you receive back from them.

2. Make immediate written notes of all conversations with rental managers or landlords relative to your complaints and their promises of attention to the problems. Keep these and date them as you go.

3. If you are forced to make repairs just to be able to keep living in the place (paying for furnace repair in the winter, getting an inoperative toilet fixed by the plumber, or hiring an electrician to make the range work), give the landlord immediate notice that you have done so, provide immediate proof of cost and also of all efforts to get the landlord to fix the problem. This includes keeping those notes of telephone calls and visits to the rental office to complain.

4. If you have to move out because of the lack of basic services like heat, water, sewer, or working appliances, give notice at once and demand return of deposits paid. *The tenant has the right to peaceful enjoyment of the property, and failure to provide these things can constitute a "constructive eviction."* This means you can maintain an action for damages, claiming the landlord effectively threw you out of the place by depriving you of these basic necessities. A woman can't care for her kids in a place with an inoperative refrigerator. It's just that simple. Almost all standard leases contain a provision promising to provide a "habitable tenancy" or words to that effect, and the case law also recognizes that principle. If you can't live in it, you don't have to pay for it. The problem is that you need to file suit to get protection. An action asking the court to award damages and declare the lease terminated for the landlord's breach of its terms is the best way to proceed, and counsel can help. Where non-reimbursement of security deposit is also an issue, attorneys' fees are collectible too. Keep records on all this stuff, as well, including pictures of bad conditions and repair or at least complaint records for the problems that made it impossible to keep living in the unit.

CHAPTER SIX
⚖ Consumer Protection Laws

G ET READY FOR THE PROVERBIAL ALPHABET SOUP OF LEGAL MUMBO JUMBO. In the past thirty years, there has probably not been more fertile ground for legislative and regulatory hysteria than in the area called "consumer protection." Often well-intentioned, usually overbroad, and always cumbersome and invasive of the relationships between consumer and producer, these laws have reached into every area of American commerce. From lending to saving and using a checking account, a vast array of bureaucratic regulations and newfound ills-to-be-cured have nearly choked the banking industry with rules intended to protect financial institution customers from those financial institutions. In the vast area of consumer products, every conceivable federal and state agency has found a way to stick its nose into the newly discovered business of telling the producers of goods what and how they can produce, market, advertise, merchandise, sell, and warrant their wares. The stock market, home sales, airline passage, dental appliances, and even computer keyboards have become targets of regulations intended in some often obscure way to "protect" us either from some capitalist or from ourselves.

There have been innumerable results from this, most of which were unintended and many of which have only made things worse. Like the stone tossed in the pool, the ripples went places no one thought about when the stone was thrown, and the impact of all this has been almost uniformly to dramatically increase the cost of every item and service we obtain in the great marketplace of America. Of course, there have been ills cured and bad things made better, as there were some in our vast economy who were always willing to take unfair advantage of the consumer, and we will discuss those in this chapter. My editorial is only intended to declare a truth that is as righteous as it is politically incorrect—that the officious, overzealous personality of the American Left has, as is its uniform practice, often used weapons of mass destruction on the entirety of commerce in the name of "protection" of consumers, in the end doing more to drive up the cost of what consumers buy than saving consumers from any perceived ill.

Let's take a short look at a number of regulations and other laws that address the area. We'll proceed with the lending-related areas first, then talk about product safety and warranties as well.

LENDING

A substantial portion of the law in this area came out of the civil rights movement and its claims of racial discrimination in the area of lending money. The practice of "red-lining" that had the effect of denying mortgage loans to people in low income areas (most of whom were black) was one of the first to get the ax from the courts, and federal statutes followed attacking the same problem. Essentially the rule from all sources is the same. One cannot be denied credit on the basis of gender, race, creed, color, or national origin. Simple stuff and a rule that a rational person would think pretty basic, but unfortunately the banking world at one time needed a boot to the backside to get this one across. The Federal Reserve System has promulgated many of the rules pursuant to authority granted by Congress, the Fed then identifying them by letter. Here are the big ones:

▶Truth-in-lending—Regulation Z

If you borrow money from any lender, they are required by federal law and this Fed regulation to provide you with an array of information about the cost and the terms of your loan agreement. Those loans are of two types, closed-end and open-end. Closed-end loans are characterized by their one-time disbursement feature, the borrower signing the note for a set amount, providing for a fixed payment schedule and getting all the money at once. These are the "big ticket" loans, for financing home or automobile purchases, boats, new furniture, or even a single cash disbursement for that European vacation. Open-end loans include all credit card arrangements and those cash advance loans you may have that let you write "checks" against a loan account whenever you need money. This kind of loan arrangement then contemplates repeated transactions, balances due that fluctuate from month to month, and payments that therefore also change over time. The differences in required disclosures are very substantial, and as a consumer, you have the right under the law to have the lender get it right. Failure to do so will result in a forfeiture of interest and, in some cases, damages in favor of the borrower. It galls me to admit it, but this regulation has served the interests of lenders as well as borrowers, because it actually prescribed the format, language, and even the placement on the page of most of these required items, so everybody can figure out *how* to get it right.

1. The closed-end disclosures are accomplished via a tabular format that is required to be in bold type and to appear across the top of the page, before any contract language. Called the "fed box," it sets out the cost of the loan using the term "finance charge," the interest rate, inclusive of all charges that the regulation defines as such, called the annual percentage rate or "APR," the total of all the payments you will make if you pay on time, and the frequency of payments.

2. Some itemization of those figures is also required, but it is very easy for a competent lawyer to discern whether or not there is a violation of these provisions. Violations are pretty rare these days, as getting it right doesn't require an advanced degree in astrophysics.

3. Open-end loans are much looser by definition, as the whole idea is for the borrower to have essentially unfettered access to the agreed credit limit. So long as the borrower does not attempt to exceed that limit and makes

the required payments on time, the open-end loan is the closest thing in all the law to a perpetual motion machine. However, the agreement must contain some of the same disclosures, although there is no stark "fed box" type requirement. The annual percentage rate must be there, along with the method of computing the finance charge and periodic payment, and the contract must also provide information regarding what to do when a card is lost or stolen. The trouble usually starts with the periodic billing statement. It must disclose the rate, the finance charge for the period, the amount of the payment required, and the total of extensions of credit during the period, among other things.

The thing to remember as a consumer in this area is that the lender is required to inform you meaningfully about the terms and costs of your loan. Failing to do that results in a violation of the regulation, and from that violation flows damages and interest forfeitures if proven. And because there are few defenses to a suit that claims failure to pay the amount due, checking the documents for possible regulatory violations may provide the only set-off or counterclaim available in defense of such a suit.

►*Fair Credit Billing*

This is actually a part of Regulation Z, but it is a separate set of rules relating to the content of your periodic statements in open-end loans. Not only are there requirements for proper periodic disclosures, there is a requirement of *re*-disclosure on an annual basis, so that the lender must send all borrowers, at least once a year, a long form disclosure of the required information. It's just the same stuff that was required in the first place, but it's in addition to what must appear on each periodic statement. Again, there are forfeitures of interest earned and other damages assessed against the lender for violating these terms. The idea is to ensure that the borrower knows what and how the lender is charging for the use of money, the terms of repayment, and amount outstanding. Chances are that if the billing statement is confusing or missing required information, the regulation has been violated. Again, just about everyone gets it right these days, because the rule has been in existence for many years, and the language of the regulation has been litigated often enough that we all read it the same way.

▶Fair Credit Reporting

This one is a mess. Virtually everyone who has ever owed money, paid taxes, or rented an apartment has had a credit bureau report experience that sounds like a horror story by Stephen King. What we will tell you here will shed some light on that dark tale, but even the high-mindedness of the Federal Trade Commission, the bureaucracy charged with writing and enforcing the Fair Credit Reporting law, has trouble harnessing this beast. You are entitled to know these things:

1. The name of any credit reporting agency (credit bureau) that reports anything negative about you when a creditor you want to borrow from seeks information.

2. Because we typically only find out about bad stuff in the report when we get turned down for credit, a new apartment, a car lease, or a re-finance on our home, that's the time to be certain to review any bad report. If you ask, they must show you the report, and it has to be free if you make the request within sixty days of learning about the bad news. You also can get one free report per year if you are unemployed, on welfare, or have information that the data in the report is wrong due to fraud. You can get one any time by paying the cost, an amount that the regulation caps at no more than $8.00.

3. When you complain about an error, the agency reporting the erroneous information must investigate your claim within thirty days. That means they go to the source of the bad data, like a report of an old delinquency, unpaid balance, judgment, or lien, and require that source to investigate your claim and change the report if it is in error. *This all sounds fine, unless you are fighting with a national*

credit card company, a huge credit bureau, or, God forbid, the IRS.

4. They are supposed to correct all erroneous information at the source, or if they disagree with your claim of error, at least make a note that appears in the credit report, stating that you dispute the bad information.

The major credit bureaus and most all the lenders doing business in a major market know this rule, and most make a reasonable effort to comply with it. However, many will turn you down on your request for credit anyway, seeking to move on to the next applicant instead of giving you the opportunity to prove the report wrong. One major exception to this is the mortgage lending area, where lenders tend to permit some investigation and often take time to assist. One of my clients has had the same state tax lien, entered in error some ten years ago, reappear at least three times on various reports after being corrected by the Indiana Department of Revenue twice. Like some computer virus that refuses to die, or one of those evil social diseases that reappears every few years at the most embarrassing times, it can be almost impossible to finally drive a stake through the monster's heart. The best thing to do at such times is to make a personal appearance at the creditor's offices and find some live body to help you fix the problem. Those automated push-button systems you get on the phone will only drive you insane, and eventually tell you they can't, *or won't* help you out. A lawyer's letterhead is very helpful here, but few lawyers have the patience or the expertise to fight this battle effectively. The big lenders and credit bureaus, as well as virtually all taxing authorities, just appear not to care much what happens to you.

Where the problem is continued reporting of an obligation that has been paid, and where that obligation was at one time delinquent, all the reporting agency will do is show it paid. They will not remove the reference to the prior delinquency, judgment, garnishment, or its resultant impact on one's credit rating. The theory is that "facts are facts" relating to your misdeeds in the prompt payment department, and even though the thing might have been cleared up by now, your payment history is still relevant to those who consider extending you credit now. One more thing is important in this area, for sure. If you know there is trouble on a report, and where that trouble is the truth, fix it before you apply for credit, or at least tell the creditor about it when you make the application. Extenuating circumstances that sometimes lead to delinquency or default will occasionally make a difference to the new lender. An extended illness, long job lay-off, injury, or even a particularly nasty divorce are all things that help explain a bad run of luck—and credit. And if you have proof of the error, or better yet, proof that the problem has been fixed by your efforts, take it and show it to the new lender at the time you make application.

If you need federal help, call the Federal Trade Commission offices in Chicago.

▶*Equal Credit Opportunity—Regulation B*

This is just what it sounds like, a rule that imposes the same prohibitions against discrimination that apply to employment situations. There can be no discrimination on the basis of race, creed, color, religion, or national origin, and a lender who does so is exposed to fines, penalties, damages, and attorneys' fees, just as is the case with Title VII of the civil rights law. Heralded by those who saw the banking world as another racist evil empire, Reg. B really never had much impact beyond heaping another bucket full of paper on the lending industry. To the surprise of very few, the federal statute and this regulation of the Federal Reserve System really produced little in the way of litigation and punishment on the money world for the simple reason that, across the board, lenders simply did not engage in discriminatory practices *as a rule*. Nevertheless, you have the right to know the reasons for any "adverse action" taken by a lender to whom you make application for an extension of credit. It typically has to be in writing, and you have to ask for it within sixty days of having been turned down on the application in question. The lender then has thirty days in which to respond, and it must identify by name the people who were responsible for the decision. Where this is a third party reporting agency, the provisions of Fair Credit Reporting also come into play. If you believe that a denial of credit has been in some degree based upon a racial or other factor, like color, creed, religion, or national origin, you can make complaint to the federal agency that regulates that institution. For banks, the Federal Deposit Insurance Corp., "FDIC"; for credit unions, the National Credit Union Administration, "NCUA"; for thrift institutions like savings banks, the Federal Savings and Loan Insurance Corp., "FSLIC"; for agricultural loans, the Farm Credit Administration, "FCA" or the Secretary of Agriculture; or if none of those, you can go to the Federal Trade Commission. Violations of this regulation are rare, and they usually consist more of technical failures like not using the right forms or not completing them the right way.

▶ *Truth-in-Savings*

This one is a real trip, and for the life of me I have never understood the reason for all the paper, expense, and hot air that went into it. The idea is simply that an institution that holds your money and pays you interest for it has to tell you the truth about the rate of interest earned and the method of calculation and crediting of that interest. It created a whole additional pile of regulatory compliance materials and an array of new forms, the whole idea of which was just to tell you your savings rates. Known as "Regulation DD," this appropriately named voluptuous gal indeed demands serious support to hold up her enormous endowment of paper and red tape. The short version of the rule is that the savings institution has the responsibility of telling you the actual rate at which your money will earn interest, to the nearest $1/100^{th}$ of a percent and the yield in dollars you will earn, based on some forms prescribed for that purpose by the Federal Reserve System. The "APY" or Annual Percentage Yield is the big deal here, and although it's a real pain in the undergarment to the banking world, knowing just what they mean when they tell you a rate is a good thing after all. If you think you have been told some wrong information about the rates and methods of calculation for your savings, take it up with the same offices listed earlier in Equal Credit Opportunity. Violations are not commonplace, as the forms prescribed by the Fed make compliance easier and more predictable.

▶ Uniform Consumer Credit Code

This law has been around for many years, the product of the era when liberal lawmakers viewed every lender, landlord, or seller of goods as a racist pig in search of an unwary and unsophisticated consumer to rape. A combination of truth-in-lending and various other federal models, it essentially imposes some of the same restrictions and disclosure requirements that are contained in other sources, plus some additional restrictions on lending rates, permissible charges that can be imposed on certain kinds of loan accounts, and even rules on personal property credit sales. This complex of definitions and regulations on credit sales and lending specifically addresses maximum interest rates, "cooling off periods" for in-home sales, and charges associated with insuring property or repayment of loan balances. This stuff is just too confusing and lengthy to try to understand without benefit of counsel, so if you suspect that you've been had by an over-aggressive lender or contract seller, get help. For those who fear that their business might include one of the areas mentioned above, it is imperative that you **get your documents reviewed for compliance with this law, as it includes some nasty penalties for those who violate its provisions.**

Consumer Protection Laws—Sale of Goods

There are a number of laws designed to protect private consumers and those involved in commerce from certain deficiencies in goods sold. The oldest is the Uniform Commercial Code, the stalwart of folks who sell things for a living and who use the banking system to make payment and establish loans to each other. We will address it briefly, as the course in law school on the UCC is sixteen weeks long and comprises some of the most important information the student lawyer learns. We will discuss the Indiana version of what is usually referred to as the "Lemon Law" here because its contents are not well known to most Hoosiers. The Lemon Law is a sort of statutory warranty rule that gives all consumer purchasers of motor vehicles a firm 18 month/18,000 mile warranty. The law applies only to manufacturers and specifically *excludes* dealers. (Guess who had a really strong lobby at the sausage factory, i.e., Indiana General Assembly.) While the language of the statute does not specify whether or not the law applies to the purchase and sale of used cars, there is no exclusion for that kind of car. So if your "new to you" car won't work, and you give reasonable opportunity to the *manufacturer* to make it work, you may have the remedy of requiring them to take it back and refund your purchase price. They get a deduction from the original price for use, but the bottom line is that they have to take it back and pay you enough money to get your car loan repaid. It makes sense to tie the "use" calculation to the amount of the monthly payment, so in the end, you should be whole. But keep in mind that there are some procedures to be followed, including timely complaint to the manufacturer, opportunity to make adequate repairs, and use of an informal procedure for working out the disagreement, and at least four separate efforts to fix the problem. One more thing—this law won't help you unless the defect actually makes the car essentially unusable. Disagreeable problems that make you nuts probably won't qualify, unless the thing makes you so batty that you can't operate it. Act in a timely fashion and keep records of your demands and the efforts of the manufacturer to cure the defect. If it all fails, demand return and refund.

▶*Uniform Commercial Code*

This old law has been the reliable source of trade and commercial reason for decades, and its footprint is all over modern rules relating to commercial transactions. For our purposes here, you should understand that its biggest application to the consumer world has to do with the sale of goods and also to the creation of debt relationships through the promissory notes we all sign when we borrow money or open a credit account. Lemon Law was nothing more than a restatement of the rules regarding express and implied warranties contained in Article 2 of the UCC. That means the same concepts about requiring products to do what they're supposed to do, used in the Lemon Law to apply to motor vehicles, also applies to dishwashers, lawn mowers, freezers, computers, fishing rods, and aspirin. Goods that are "nonconforming" in their condition or capacity to do what they were sold to do can be returned or the seller forced to make them right. Without getting too technical, just remember this rule: **There is an implied warranty of merchantability and fitness for intended purposes attached by the UCC to every sale of goods in the ordinary course of business.** If the thing you buy won't work, or won't work well enough to do what you bought it to do, the seller breaches this implied warranty, and unless they make it right, they can be liable to you for damages incurred because of that nonconformity. So if the lawn mower runs but not well enough to cut the grass like you need it to, dies all the time, or is too weak to cut heavier growth, the implied warranty of fitness for particular purpose may have been breached. And if they can't make it do what you need it to do, they have to take it back and refund your money. These days, most of the bigger retailers will do just that, as it is easier to replace the offending gizmo than to mess with repairs and the predictable tantrums of irate consumers who are angry over the item's failure to work properly even after attempts to fix it. One more thing—all the limitations in the world will not overcome this warranty if you buy the thing from someone engaged in the business of selling that kind of merchandise. They can limit the kind of damages for which they might be liable, but the warranties of merchantability and fitness for purpose are powerful medicine that continue to protect us all, although most of us don't really know they're there. It is permissible under the law to issue disclaimers that avoid the application of these warranties, and you will see them in almost every "limited warranty" that accompanies the things you buy. These are at least facially effective, but obviously the argument over whether or not the thing is what the seller said it was still can get you a foothold in the courtroom. Those disclaimers are strictly construed against the merchants/manufacturers who issue them, so the issue is certainly worth raising, especially where personal injury or serious property damage has been caused by the offending widgit.

CHAPTER SEVEN
⚖ Creditors' Rights and Bankruptcy

THE COMMERCIAL STRUGGLES BETWEEN THOSE WHO LEND MONEY AND THOSE who borrow it moved into the legislative arena back in the 1960s and changed the way people did business in this area for all time. For hundreds of years before the advent of the Uniform Commercial Code, folks in Western Europe and America lent and borrowed money on the basis of convention and court precedent that heavily favored the lender, but which made certain rules hard and fast in protection of those who owed accounts. However, in the social revolution of the 1960s most of that changed, as what was perceived as the excesses of the banking system came under attack.

That alphabet soup of regulations we addressed in the chapter on consumer protection was the big piece to the lending revolution, but even with the hard Left turn that was signaled by all those changes, the lender still emerged from the war with at least a nominal right to get paid back—sometimes. Of course I'm being a bit facetious, but it still seems to this old lawyer that what the social revolutionaries from the far Left wanted was for everyone to get money from the lenders whenever they wanted, but never to have to pay any of it back. The big problem with that one is that pretty soon the cash is gone—and so is the lender.

COLLECTIONS

All modern-day consumer debt is created in writing, no matter what we call it, and that document, whether it's a promissory note, a credit card or other revolving credit agreement, a lease, or even a "lease-to-own" type deal will control any dispute. *Debt can be created without a document, as where one person simply loans money or sells a car to another on a handshake and promise to pay, but we are concerned here with the kind of debt that is created in the marketplace between consumers and commercial lenders or sellers of goods.* The language of all those different kinds of documents has a few common characteristics that make them what they are—written evidence of a debt and an obligation to pay it back. Let's look at what happens when a consumer fails to follow the requirements of that language.

The term "default" is a legal term of art that includes many things, but all of them constitute a breach of the borrower's responsibilities. (Obviously a lender can also default but most of those liabilities are set out in the consumer protection discussion.) The most obvious borrower default is of course a failure to pay on time and in the amount required by the deal. Others include failing to maintain insurance on property pledged as collateral for repayment of the loan or permitting a car or other collateral to be used for an illegal purpose, to get torn up, or to lose possession of it. For example, it is a default under a car loan to permit the car to get lost so that the borrower no longer has possession of it or even knows where it is. I once was involved in a collection case for a credit union that had lost its interest in a motorcycle because the borrower had lost it, and the guy who ended up with it signed a false affidavit with the BMV that permitted him to take title and also to give a lien to a different lender as well! Ouch. We default on our obligations on real estate mortgages when we fail to maintain the property in good condition or when we fail to keep the property adequately insured with a policy that provides for the proceeds to go to the lender in the event of fire or other casualty. In short, it's just a good idea to read the default provisions for your loans, because there are a number of trip wires there that can get you sideways with your creditor.

When one fails to pay or otherwise to keep up with the terms of the loan agreement, the lender has the right to call the whole balance due. A failure to make a payment does not just expose the borrower to a claim for the amount of that payment, because the agreements all have "acceleration clauses" that cause the entire amount outstanding to become due when you default at all. That's one of the reasons folks get so messed up on car or mortgage loans sometimes. Once a creditor has claimed an acceleration, school's out and the whole banana is owed. Let's address that specific problem a bit; so many folks get all messed up on home mortgage liabilities and car loans because they don't understand this concept well.

When a payment is made late, the computer-driven accounting programs of the lender immediately flag the account as delinquent. Two things happen at that point:

1. The account gets put into a special status that causes the accounting software to spit out a delinquency notice that *also* advises the credit bureau that you haven't made your payments on time. This only happens after the delinquency gets longer in duration or has happened repeatedly, as when you make late payments on several occasions.

2. A delinquency fee gets added to the loan balance and also is added to the amount due on the next payment. Pay attention here, because this is where the details hide the devil, big time. You're late in month one, and the contract provides for a 10% late charge to be added to the next payment and also the loan balance. You pay on time in month two, but you don't notice the late fee on the monthly statement and only pay the usual contract amount in that month. So you still just owe the late fee, right? *WRONG. For as long as that late fee remains unpaid, you will remain delinquent and therefore the length of your default will continue to grow.* So if you pay on time in month three but again fail to pay the late charge, the computer keeps on showing you delinquent, now not just for the one you made late, but *FOR ALL THREE!* What a mess. Of course in the car loan business, being down three months is often plenty of delinquency to produce an order from the collections people at the bank for repossession of your car. Now most won't order a repo on the basis of a missed late fee alone, but the chance exists, and the contract clearly permits it if they want to play hardball. **A special note here on mortgage loans. When you're late and incur a late fee on your mortgage, many lenders will refuse to credit later payments**

in subsequent months at all until the fees are paid. They will hold your subsequent payments in escrow, waiting to credit them toward your balance until the fees are paid. Interest on the outstanding balance continues to accrue, each payment they hold in escrow is viewed as not made at all, and delinquency fees pile up for each month on those later payments until all are paid up. I recently had a client amass over $10,000 in charges and extra interest over a mess like this, and the account got referred to the lawyers for foreclosure before we unraveled the whole thing, costing him about two grand in lender's attorneys' fees as well. To make matters worse in the mortgage arena, the loans are often not serviced by the institution that wrote the loan in the first place, and you have to wade through a whole platoon of uninterested, sometimes difficult and always difficult-to-contact people who live in some faraway place. The best answer is not to be late and to pay close attention to communications from mortgage lenders or those with whom you have a car loan. In addition to all the hassles described above, a long problem with either of those institutions will almost certainly show up as a bad rating from them on your credit report.

After being accelerated under the terms of the agreement, most lenders spend little time on collecting the money themselves before at least assigning the claim to an agency. These are the guys who send the computer-generated mail that contains the threats of suit, damage to credit, or loss of property if "further proceedings" are required. The federal Fair Debt Collections Act kicks in here, requiring a string of disclosures and regulating the conduct of outside collection agencies and attorneys hired to recover outstanding balances. While it is a relatively silly overkill, like we've come to expect in this age of rampant consumerism, its provisions are powerful and can cause a creditor to lose real money if the terms of the statute are not followed. Moreover, penalties and damages are specified in the law that hit both agencies and lawyers right between the eyes. Bottom-feeding at its best . . . the most obvious piece to all this is the requirement of a particular notice on all communications to a debtor by anyone other than in-house employees of the creditor. That notice must advise the debtor that the letter in his hands is an attempt to collect a debt and also tell him what to do to contest the claims being made. While violations of these requirements, like truth-in-lending or equal credit opportunity errors, can give rise to counter-claims on behalf of the debtor in a law suit to collect the money owed, most of the time the lender has a pretty easy time of getting a judgment for the amount owed, plus accrued interest, fees, court costs, and attorneys' fees. Fees for the lawyer who collects the money on behalf of the creditor are provided for in virtually every loan agreement, subject only to laws that limit them in some states. In Indiana, the fees are not permitted to be flat or based solely on a contingency or percentage of the amount of the judgment. The courts assess fees based upon time the lawyer puts into the individual case.

Debtors seldom win in these cases, but the value of having counsel where the amount is substantial is pretty obvious. Being able to raise the specter of these counterclaims for regulatory or collections violations can make a huge difference in the outcome of the case. It is important that the debtor has a lawyer who is skilled in the contents and application of this alphabet soup of federal and state debtor protection law.

▶Judgment

When you lose to a creditor in a collection case, the court enters a judgment that entitles that creditor to repayment of all amounts awarded by the court. Just a quick list of what this means to the judgment debtor:

1. Garnishment. After notice and a hearing, the creditor's lawyer can institute a garnishment of the wages of those who owe the money. This garnishment is handled by the court on the basis of a formula that is derived from a multiple of the minimum wage at the time, so that not all the wages or salary of the debtor are subject to the order. This takes the form of an order against the debtor's employer,

requiring the payment of a portion of the net wages to the court for application against the amount awarded in the judgment. The only effective way to avoid this eventuality for the debtor is to make a voluntary arrangement with the creditor's lawyer for payments to be made, *and then to make them as promised without fail.* If you make promises but don't keep them, almost every collection lawyer in the world will refuse to deal with you anymore.

2. Levy of Execution. Non-exempt property that is not covered by a security interest in favor of another creditor can be taken and sold. The sheriff seizes things like cars or other personal property and sells them at auction. The proceeds are then applied to the judgment. This also applies to real estate in cases where the only people who have an interest in the property are also the judgment debtors. We'll address exemptions for one's homestead later in the section on bankruptcy, but one thing to remember is that the debts of one spouse do not attach to the interests of both in real estate. This is not the case with personal property, including accounts, but as to real property, a judgment against one spouse is not a judgment against both, and the claims of a creditor of one (not both) cannot be satisfied out of the real estate interests both hold together as husband and wife. So a judgment against Dad will not permit a judgment creditor to seize and sell real property owned by Dad *and* Mom. But if both are sued and judgment is taken against both, the property of both is susceptible to the claims of that creditor.

3. Bank Accounts. Using about the same procedure for obtaining a wage garnishment, creditors are permitted to garnish—actually to take—accounts held in the names of those against whom they have judgment. But unlike the wage garnishment that has built into it an exemption for a portion of the earned income per week, a bank account garnishment will result in the entire balance in the ac-

count being taken for application to the judgment. That one is really painful for the debtor, and the only way to avoid it is to either keep accounts secret, close them and do business in cash, put all accounts in the name of a non-involved spouse only, or make peace with the creditor before the hammer falls. There is a long-standing exemption for social security payments that have been deposited into an account, and when you can prove those proceeds are in the account in question, the court will order the funds returned.

4. Set-off. If you are unlucky enough to end up owing a delinquent obligation to the same bank where you have your savings or checking accounts the bank can simply exercise its common law right of set-off and take as much of your money from those accounts as it takes to satisfy its claims without any court intervention at all. So if you're in trouble, you can see that it's a really bad idea to continue maintaining accounts in the same institution where you're in the bag for a delinquent obligation. Best move the accounts.

BANKRUPTCY—CHAPTER 13

The ultimate weapon in the war between debtors and creditors is the bankruptcy petition. Billions of dollars per year in consumer debt are washed away by these proceedings, and for the most part there is no countermeasure that is effective against it. Once upon a time, there was a strong social and financial stigma attached to the word "bankrupt" that left the debtor damaged by the process, even though he or she was absolved of those obligations by the court's decree. So much of that has changed now, and so many more folks have been through it, that much of that negative aspect to the whole process has disappeared. Creditors actively court the recently bankrupt, competing to help them get right back in the same quicksand that destroyed their economic wellbeing as in the past. Of course the interest rates they experience will hit them like a falling building, and the collateral required may be pretty extensive, but the credit will be there for sure.

Not all is rosy for the person who has been baptized at the bankruptcy font, as there are still merchants, landlords, and lenders who require extra precaution when dealing with those who have demonstrated poor financial skills. Getting an apartment may require a cosigner who guarantees the rental obligation in the event of default or eviction. A spouse may be an attractive additional party where the couple owns property that might be pledged as security for the loan—or be snatched and sold in the event of judgment. And as silly as it sounds, I have often counseled clients whom we've taken through bankruptcy to try to establish credit again on some limited basis as soon as possible. While we also caution them about the pitfalls of getting extended again, we feel, particularly where single women are concerned, that re-establishing credit and building a good history of timely payments is an important ingredient in the process of starting over. Single moms who dream of having a home for their kids but who have been through bankruptcy in the throes of a divorce need to start developing their own financial identity. Mortgage lenders tend to be the most cautious here, as the amount of money involved is usually much larger than that associated with apartment rent, a credit card limit, or even a car loan obligation. With all that said, it is still my belief that bankruptcy hurts those who use it, both financially and also with matters of community reputation, although not to the extent that once was true. The law calls it the "fresh start" concept, and truly it can be such, but just be aware that it's not a decision to be made lightly.

Bankruptcy is another of those areas where people often try to go without counsel. There are "kits" available for preparing and filing your own petition with the court, and truthfully, many cases where there are no assets and few if any secured creditors to mess up the works can slide through without a hitch even with no lawyer to assist. My one question would be that if your financial woes are so simple that you can dispose of them yourself without the assistance of counsel, are they simple enough for you to solve in some other less drastic and damaging way? Numerous consumer credit counseling operations exist in almost every city and town, and these people can deal with creditors to establish reduced payment plans and forbearance against repossession and even foreclosure if the debtors will work hard to keep their end of the deal. Here is a short list of things to consider before jumping off the bridge:

1. Know the details of who and what you owe, from the name of the creditor, to the mailing address, balance due, and even the account number for every one. Write them all down and collect a statement, demand letter, or payment book for each, so there is a way to verify the accuracy of every obligation to be listed in the petition. This will also help you with this next suggestion.

2. Take the list, along with your checkbook or other records of your personal finances, your record of income for the current and prior year, and your tax returns to your accountant, lawyer, parent, minister, or some other person you trust. Go over the whole mess with that person to determine whether or not you really need to use the ultimate weapon. Advice from one of those aforementioned counseling services is usually free, and they will propose a plan to help you get out of the trouble without taking the plunge. Only when it is clear after that kind of consideration that there is no other way out do you want to move ahead with bankruptcy.

3. Be sure the result of that list is proof of "no way out." If the list of bad news is shorter than you thought, it may make sense to approach the creditors you do have and seek arrangements that permit you to dig out of the hole over time. Too often folks bale out because they think there's no other way, but the problem is only a couple of creditors who are more demanding or less reasonable than the rest. Help from family or a bill consolidation loan might make the difference, especially if you can make a deal with the mortgage company or car lender who has security that is crucial to your future.

4. First thing to do when you find yourself in a hole is to stop digging. If there are features to your economic life

that got you into trouble, consider dropping them. Hobbies, activities, even associations that have too much expense associated with them can be at least suspended, if not abandoned. Folks come in to counsel with a long list of toys that cost too much to maintain, then are surprised they need to file bankruptcy. Boats, motorcycles, airplanes, hunting, fishing, skiing, or other sporting pastimes are expensive and cost a ton to keep up. It may be possible to sell off some of the non-essential stuff, apply the proceeds to the biggest problem debts, then use the extra income available from losing the payments to apply toward other obligations. One guy ended up in divorce *and* bankruptcy because of a combination of gambling habits and a huge passion for golf. It was a high price to pay for things so frivolous. The guy even got behind on his *non-dischargeable* child support because of these silly items. In that case we represented his wife in the divorce proceeding, and needless to say, we treated him to a permanent vacation in the fine art of reality on planet Earth.

5. For families with their own homes, there may be equity in the residence (appraised value in excess of the mortgage balance) that could help stop the financial bleeding if it were tapped. We do not recommend second mortgages—the famous "home equity loan"—because that just creates another monthly obligation. Instead, if you've owned the place for a while, the payments made plus the natural increase in value that is typical for most homes around Indiana will have created some equity. A new mortgage, refinanced and used to pay off the old one, will provide two very important features that can help you avoid taking the fall:

a. Proceeds can be applied to past-due accounts, paying off existing loan balances or bringing current obligations that you can't pay off.

b. The new mortgage will probably have a lower monthly payment, because you will be extending the balance out over a new thirty-year term. If the market is good for interest rates at the time, that will also drive down the monthly payment, to the extent you are able to do the refinance at a lower rate than the old loan.

Note: Selling boats, motor homes, motorcycles, or other toys may leave a shortfall against the outstanding balance, so that, even without the item in your garage, you still have a payment to make. If there is equity in the home, it can be applied to that net balance so you end up with fewer payments each month.

6. With or without adding income from a second job, sending Mom back to work, or the like, a new, strict budget is essential. Cutting frills is painful for the moment, but it can bear the best results if you stick to it. And believe it or not, as bad as money problems are for a marriage, working and sacrificing together in this way actually can help repair those frayed connections the cash shortage started. And in this era of excess and children who know little of sacrifice, the lesson is never lost on them. Coming through a tough financial time after letting go of unimportant items or habits can be the best training and lessons a kid can get.

7. Finally, pick someone to represent you who will spend the time to make sure you get it right. A bankruptcy that fails to list all creditors, or worse, fails to avoid the liens of old judgments or tax claims, is worse than no bankruptcy at all. My partner insists that his paralegal personally interview each potential client to go over the painful details of his or her financial picture. The good lawyers have questionnaires that elicit every stitch of information about the financial condition of the debtors, and that kind of attention to detail is essential for the whole thing to work. The idea of bankruptcy is to create a "fresh start" for the debtor who's in the hole; that can't happen if creditors are left out. Even those you intend to reaffirm and keep must be

listed, and you can then work with them after filing. But failing to list them all is a cardinal sin from which there may be no escape later.

▶Bankruptcy Fraud ·

Everyone should have a healthy respect for this one. Back during the early years of the "new and improved" bankruptcy code, debtors and their lawyers could do some pretty creative things. There were a few years back in the late 1970s and early 1980s when folks were getting discharged from their debts just because they were tired of making payments. And during this time the courts began to see more and more efforts to use the liberal rules of the code to accomplish ends that were simply unacceptable to them. Now the requirements of full disclosure and cooperation have become much more stringent.

The days of "forgetting" assets, pending court settlements, distributions from decedents' estates, and deferred compensation packages are long gone, and those who fail to make full and complete disclosure of all their property can expect to get in major hot water. And beyond just hiding assets, actions taken by debtors or their lawyers to use the bankruptcy court as a shield against creditors—things like repetitive filings followed by dismissals, failing to file required schedules and other requirements—have landed many in the federal penitentiary. *It is imperative that we remember this: seeking relief from the bankruptcy court is serious business, and it requires detailed and forthright disclosure of all aspects of one's financial condition.* Bankruptcy fraud catches more and more people who seek to play fast and loose with the disclosure requirements of the act, and getting caught can have enormous consequences.

LIQUIDATION—CHAPTER 7

This one is truly the "ultimate plunge." One who files a Chapter 7 bankruptcy action is throwing in the towel and asking the court to discharge him from all obligations. Upon the filing of a petition declaring that the debtor is indeed insolvent, "unable to meet his obligations as they come due," the court issues that same "automatic stay" of all proceedings and actions to collect any debt, and everything has to stop until the first meeting of creditors occurs. This operates just like the one in the Chapter 13 proceeding, and even mortgage foreclosures, in addition to sheriff's sales, garnishments, levies, and state court receiverships are stayed by the order. Here is a sketch of what happens during this period, including the end result:

1. Money held by banks under garnishment or attachment orders from state courts is typically not recoverable by the trustee or the debtors if the order and seizure occurred before the bankruptcy was filed. In order to avoid this result, the debtor must file the petition before the money is taken. The order for garnishment is stayed, however, so the necessity of moving is obvious.

2. Secured creditors who have initiated repossession actions must stop them, and they are guilty of contempt of court if they seize cars or other property after the stay is issued.

3. Real estate foreclosure actions and even sheriff's sales must cease action until the bankruptcy judge lifts the stay. This can be crucial for those whose financial or personal situation has deteriorated to the point where loss of their residence is eminent.

4. Every creditor will receive a notice of the bankruptcy filing, and that notice will instruct them to stop all collection action. Continuation of collection efforts can also result in contempt of court, and the courts have little sympathy for those who commit such an error. The result of all this is a sort of deafening silence, following the months or years of screeching from the ever-burgeoning pack of creditors who often hound debtors as things get worse and worse.

5. The first meeting of creditors follows this period of quiet,

the time when all who would raise some complaint about their security or the assets of the debtor can do so. The courts appoint interim trustees, lawyers who conduct these meetings after having first reviewed the debtor's petition and accompanying paperwork. Those who want to resume efforts to foreclose security interests, including creditors who had repossessed cars or other property at the time the automatic stay was issued but had not sold them yet, can seek "relief from the stay." The trustee will hear those matters at the first meeting or at least attempt to resolve those issues, and it is then that the debtor's lawyer earns his keep. Those who filed because they wanted to keep their homes or cars (often already the subject of recovery proceedings in state court at the time) must act quickly and deal fairly with those creditors if arrangements are to be made in that regard.

The debtor was required to list all property owned or in which even a partial interest was held at the time of the filing of the bankruptcy, and the trustee looks at all that information before the first meeting. He is looking for the following:

a. non-exempt property ownership that can be liquidated for payment to the debtor's creditors, including interests in real estate, accounts, vehicles, or other property that might be sold

b. claims against third parties that might yield funds for payments to creditors. This includes pending lawsuits for personal injury or any other kind of damages, interests in pending decedents' estates (where an inheritance might be realized), tax refunds in excess of the amount of cash permitted to be exempted from the claims of creditors, unpaid income, commissions, deferred compensation, or even interest on an investment that had not been paid

c. any likelihood that the insolvency of the debtor can be expected to be short-term or temporary, as when due to a lay-off or other job action that will end soon. Wherever possible, they will try to get the Chapter 7 debtor into a Chapter 13 proceeding, as the courts prefer that debtors make the effort to pay their creditors instead of discharging all obligations without payment

d. any evidence of fraud or other mischief demonstrating an attempt by the debtor to hide assets from the court and creditors. This one is dangerous, and everyone should be advised that bankruptcy fraud is big, serious business. Folks who try it and get caught can expect to spend time as the guest of the Bureau of Prisons over at that garden spot of a penitentiary in Terre Haute.

The first meeting is the big event in most cases, and the vast majority of issues regarding cars and residences is resolved there. More is accomplished out in the hallways than in the meeting itself, as the lawyers who do this type of work typically know each other and have developed enough understanding of what the trustee and the court will do to be able to figure out the best course by agreement. But remember this: *Follow-up is essential. Promises made by debtors and their lawyers that don't come true after the first meeting can be disastrous for the folks who are eager to keep secured property—like their cars or homes.* Creditors lose patience quickly with those who promise reaffirmation agreements or cash payments to cure defaults but then fail to deliver. Whatever you say you will do, it is absolutely essential that you follow through.

6. After the first meeting has taken place, the agreements or arrangements made by the parties must be reduced to writing, and the most common document that does so is the "Reaffirmation Agreement." The bankruptcy code permits free and voluntary agreement for continued obligation by debtors who would otherwise receive a discharge of indebtedness on particular claims. So you can say to

the lender who has an interest in your car or house that you want to keep paying, cure default as agreed, if you can keep the property that secures the loan. These are governed by specific rules relating to whether or not they are truly voluntary, the relationship between the balance being reaffirmed, and the value of the property being retained by the debtor and the presence of advice of counsel. There is even a sort of "Miranda warning" that the debtor must acknowledge receiving and an acknowledgement by the lawyer that he has advised them of the consequences of the new deal. What is important to understand is that the reaffirmation will cause the debt to survive the whole proceeding, and any subsequent default will certainly result in loss of the property *and collection of a deficiency judgment.* There lies the rub. A real mess can result if folks make a bad deal at this point. Assume for a moment that the debtor really wants to keep the family car, in this case a 1995 Oldsmobile worth about $3,500. The creditor holds a lien on the title that permits it to repossess and sell the car in the event of default, and there is little chance the car would bring that much on the auction block in a repo sale. The loan is past due several months by the time the reaffirmation agreement is signed and the debtor starts paying again, so default charges, penalties, and the like accrued on the account. The car loses value quickly at that age, so if the debtor eventually falls behind again and the car is sold at auction, there is no way the car will bring a big enough price to pay off the balance. So the creditor, after repossession and sale, files suit for the remaining balance, plus interest, repossession costs, and attorneys' fees, leaving the debtor back in the same mess he was in when he filed his bankruptcy in the first place. Good reason to think seriously about keeping such items at the time the reaffirmation is being considered.

7. Finally, after the trustee has issued his report and declaration that there are no assets worth pursuing on behalf

of creditors, and after any creditor actions have been completed the court will issue a written "Discharge of Debtor" that does just that—absolves the petitioner of all the debts not reaffirmed during the proceeding and closing the case. This is the action and the date that will eventually show up on the debtor's credit bureau reports, showing that the proceeding was actually completed and the debts discharged.

▶*Creditor Actions to Avoid Discharge of Debts*

Besides all the actions and paperwork described above, there are proceedings inside the bankruptcy that can make a mess out of a debtor's efforts to get shed of his obligations. There are several things a debtor can do *before the petition is filed* that can come back to haunt him and the lawyer later. Where a debtor has done things intentionally that defeat the claims of creditors or that may have caused a creditor to advance funds based upon lies or other misdeeds of the debtor, if the creditor acts in a timely manner he or she can challenge the discharge of the debtor as to his or her obligation. The provisions of the act that deal with all this are complex and confusing and have enough exceptions to make the examination of them a nightmare, and even keep the lawyers who work with them spinning. Here are a few examples of things that can get you in hot water with the court.

1. Taxes owing that are less than three years old (from "date of assessment") when the petition was filed.

2. Money advanced to the debtor where the debtor lied about some relevant portion of his financial condition. This one is really sticky, and the exceptions almost consume the rule, but suffice it to say for our purposes here that you can get into a mess if you

    a. failed to list significant debts when you applied for a loan, and the debts you failed to list would have made you ineligible for the money

b. misrepresented your financial condition on a financial statement you gave a lender to induce them to make you a loan

c. misrepresented the nature or extent of obligations you had when you made application for a loan

d. told them you had clear title to property being offered as collateral at a time when you either had no interest in it or had less of an interest than you said you did

e. were intent on using the money for a particular purpose when that statement was untrue.

A huge number of cases were litigated under this provision of the act over several years, and the debtors were successful in winning enough of them that this provision sees less application than once was true. But be aware that lying or misrepresenting your financial condition to a prospective creditor can get you in major league trouble in a bankruptcy proceeding.

3. A balance of over $1,000 to any one creditor for nonessential "luxury" items, incurred within sixty days of the filing of the petition.

4. Cash advances totaling more than $1,000 that are accumulated within sixty days of the filing of the petition (*these two are referred to as "loading up" or "grossing up" provisions that, for obvious reasons, try to keep people who are going to file from filling their pockets—and closets—with a lender's money, then extending them the cold hand of fellowship in the form of a notice in bankruptcy*).

5. Student loans that are or have been guaranteed by the federal government. These are tricky, because, although they are specifically excepted from discharge by the act, where the debtor can prove that such a ruling would work a serious financial hardship on the them, the court can

still discharge the debt.

6. Alimony, child support, or spousal maintenance can all be non-dischargeable. The reasons for this one are obvious, and one can expect no charity from the court where a debtor is attempting to discharge such a claim.

7. Debts incurred because of intentional wrongdoing that results from willful or malicious misconduct. This has to do with claims for injuries one commits or damages suffered by others from criminal or near-criminal conduct.

8. Injuries caused by the debtor as the result of the operation of a motor vehicle while under the influence of drugs or alcohol.

We'll provide a copy of this portion of the bankruptcy law at the back of the book, so you can get a feel for these proceedings yourself, but suffice it to say that the just-mentioned list includes things the bankruptcy court will likely not permit to be discharged. Some lawyers think it's easier and better to litigate claims like this in the bankruptcy forum, as the rules, some believe, tend to favor the debtor there. We've tried a ton of these, both as creditors and as counsel for debtors, and that difference is minimal.

▶ Property that is Exempt from the Claims of Creditors

After all the detail addressed it should be clear that bankruptcy can be a pretty technical, confusing thing. Well get ready, because the whole area of exemptions is just as bad. Federal law sets out a whole array of property types and values that are to be exempt from the claims of creditors and of the claims of the trustee, so long as they fit the definitions and the value constraints in the law. But to make things a bit more complicated, the bankruptcy code makes provision for the individual states to choose between their own debtor exemption laws and those of the federal act, and there are even some "mix and match" possibilities stirring things up even more.

The whole idea of exemptions for debtors—ensuring that folks don't lose their ability to keep a roof over their heads and make a living—goes back hundreds of years, and is essentially just a humanitarian concept. Of course, none of these rules we'll address applies to the secured interests of mortgage lenders or others who hold purchase money liens against real or personal property. So if the debtor owes his mortgage company or the credit union car lender, these exemptions won't shield any of the value of either from those creditors' claims. Instead, the result is to keep the unsecured creditors from taking everything, leaving the debtor without the means of supporting self or dependents. The rules are, in the first instance, state law rules, and they apply to all collection actions under state law. The concept is then applied to the same ideas in the bankruptcy forum, and the values we set out here are the ones that apply:

1. Equity in the residence of the debtor, up to $7,500 for each spouse, is exempt. This means that unsecured creditors and the trustee cannot get their hands on that amount of equity, even when their claims exceed that amount. This rule permits folks to get through the big plunge with their home intact and enough equity to start over—the whole idea behind our bankruptcy laws in the first place. This exemption also applies to interests in condominium units and various "cooperative" housing interests as well as mobile or modular units that constitute the primary residence of the debtor or the debtor's dependents. Although we will discuss a $10,000 maximum limit below, it is still possible for married couples to exempt a total of $15,000 worth of residential real estate value if they both file bankruptcy. The same amount applies to exemptions from the claims of creditors in state court collection proceedings.

2. Up to $4,000 in personal property or other real estate, besides that which we mentioned above as family residence for debtor or dependents, is exempt. This figure is instead of some pretty liberal numbers provided for in the federal option, where all manner of additional categories can be exempted. However, for those who file in Indiana, those more extreme choices are not available. The reason for this one is that the bankruptcy act specifically provided

for each state to have the option to use the federal exemptions or to choose to apply their own. Indiana so chose, and our exemption options are much less expansive.

3. There's a cap on the entire amount any individual debtor can shield from the claims of his creditors, whether in bankruptcy or in a state court collection proceeding, and that is a total of $10,000. So if you have equity in your real estate of $7,500 and also have $10,000 value in personal property, you are still limited to only a total of $10,000. The rest is nonexempt and can be taken by the trustee and sold for payment to creditors. But note this: items of value to you, and even with a "fair market value" in excess of the limits we have set out here, may not interest the trustee in bankruptcy *or a judgment creditor's lawyer in a state court collection action.* Unless such things can be easily sold and converted to cash, they have little value to creditors or trustees. As you can see, there are ways to come through the big federal remedy without losing much, besides some measure of pride. It's also pretty obvious from all this that having a good lawyer who understands how all this fits together is imperative.

4. The Indiana statute also provides for the exemption of any and all legally qualified pension or other retirement accounts, so long as they are made up of funds that were not taxable when first deposited in the account. This will apply to just about all older IRAs and all 501(k) accounts as well as the bigger pension and retirement accounts often provided by larger employers. **There are no dollar limitations on these accounts, so whatever is in them is exempt.**

5. Indiana has one more little one. "Intangible personal property" totaling only $100 is also referred to in the law as "choses in action." This is most typically things like small savings accounts or capital stock of any kind. It is just so small as to be of no consequence to most folks.

It is extremely important to understand how the residential assets of married couples are treated. Mom and Dad can exempt a total of $15,000 in real estate or personal property that is used as a primary family residence in actions under state law where both are judgment debtors or in bankruptcy where both have filed. And all real estate held as "tenants by the entireties"—that unique way the law views jointly held property inside a marriage—is completely exempt from the claims of all creditors of either spouse, unless those creditors have judgment against both of you. So when Dad's business venture goes sour and he suffers a judgment from the creditors of that business, the family farm is not subject to the claims of those creditors unless Mom also signed on the debts or in some way guaranteed them. And if Dad has to take the federal remedy because of those debts, the trustee will have no claim to the value of that real estate held by the marriage, no matter how valuable it is. One client of mine lost his center of gravity *twice* over a period of years, all the while continuing to live with wife and kids in the same residence. The mortgage always got paid, the equity grew and the value went up, so that the last bankruptcy—his second—saw him exempt that property at over $50,000. And this was simply because Mom was never obligated on any of the business venture debts, and all entireties property was therefore exempt.

The law also provides for exemptions on interests in health and medical devices and aids reasonably required for the maintenance of either the debtor or any dependents. Some of these have limitations on them, so the only way to know what is best is to seek counsel.

▶ Consumer Reorganization Plans

More and more inquiries arise about the financial condition of debtors who seek liquidation of all their property (usually none at all) and discharge of all their debts. We include at the end of the book a copy of the bankruptcy information sheet now given to every petitioner in bankruptcy, and as you can see, it includes specific reference to avoiding the Chapter 7 proceeding. Moreover, at the first meeting of creditors in all Chapter 7s, the trustee questions debtor and lawyer alike concerning their familiarity with that form. What the courts and their trustees are seeking is the opportunity to funnel as many people out of Chapter 7 and into Chapter 13 as possible—and with just cause. The Chapter 13 proceeding is built around the idea that folks should pay their debts, or at least as many of their debts as they can, with the assistance of the wage earner structure. Here is how it works.

When the bankruptcy petition is filed, it contains all the same disclosures and lists of debts and assets as in the Chapter 7. In addition, there is a responsibility on the debtor to propose a plan for at least partial repayment of the debts in existence at the time the proceeding is commenced. This does not have to be completed when the petition is filed, but it must be done by the time of the first meeting of creditors, set by the court. The automatic stay is issued just like in the Chapter 7, giving the debtors immediate relief from collection actions, garnishments, foreclosure proceedings, and the like. But unlike the Chapter 7, the debtor then proposes to pay to the trustee a set portion of monthly income, and the plan describes how that money is to be divided between the creditors. Secured claims get a better bite of the pie, as do taxing authorities, but even secured creditors can be forced to accept less than the full amount due, where the fair market value is less than that amount. This is a power called "cram-down." Creditors often think of it more as a cram *up*, or even a cram *in*, but you get the idea. Predictably, taxes cannot be reduced if they are still collectible.

Once a plan has been confirmed and approved by the Chapter 13 trustee and the court, it is up to the debtors to make the proposed payment each month, and to do so on time. If they keep up their end of the bargain, they get these benefits:

1. No creditor can initiate or maintain an action to collect against them on any obligation that was included in the plan or was in existence at the time the petition was filed.

2. Debtors can reinstate delinquent mortgage obligations over an extended period—up to thirty-six or even forty months—a move that is impossible outside of Chapter 13 bankruptcy.

3. The provisions of Chapter 13 can permit the debtor to get taxing authorities off his or her back, allowing them an extended period—up to sixty months—to pay tax claims. During this time portions of the claims will not accrue further interest. This one can be huge, as the IRS has a nasty habit of finding ways to gross up its claims, adding interest to penalties, penalties to interest, fines to both, and well, it can be pretty ugly. In point of fact, it is typical for the amount of tax to be only a fraction of the amount claimed by the "revenuers" with the rest being any one or a combination of those other ways to confiscate as much of your money as they can.

4. The debtors get to keep and use all secured property, including their cars, residence, tools, household goods, and the like covered by any pledge that existed at the time the petition was filed. And no one can take action to get the stuff away from them as long as they continue to tender payment on time to the court each month.

5. The debtors can also get back property that was repossessed but not yet sold before the action was commenced. This one is stickier, but it can be done in situations where the debtors can provide adequate assurances that the secured interest of the creditor will not be damaged by letting the debtor have the item back.

6. Interest and accrued penalties that grossed up the balance can be waived or at least reduced from the prior outstanding balance on any obligation.

7. The plan can provide for less than 100% pay out of amounts due on certain obligations, and an eventual discharge of substantial portions of the debts can be obtained. This is huge, as the whole amount survives the proceeding if the debtor has chosen a liquidation instead of a consumer reorganization. This is another one of those places where good planning and the advice of competent counsel is imperative.

121

121121

8. The size of payments can be reduced by the plan, so the debtors end up with more disposable income per month than was the case before the Chapter 13 was filed, both because of the decreased payment under the plan and because of the reduction in the amount of the obligation the court approves.

9. Cosigners who do not also file bankruptcy are protected against having creditors attempt to collect from them, so long as the plan so provides and also for only so long as the debtor continues to perform as ordered. This is huge for those who have debts that have been guaranteed by family or friends; these folks were facing the same fate as that of the debtors before.

10. Student loans are always a problem in bankruptcy, because they get special treatment as government insured obligations. But in a Chapter 13 proceeding the debtor can extend payments over as long as sixty additional months, and the size of the payments can be reduced as well. This provision can be big where student loans are a significant portion of the debt load. Being able to sustain payments and still have some kind of a life is a huge break for those who are in up to their ears.

The results of the successful completion of this kind of arrangement are much better for the future credit rating and creditworthiness of debtors than those where a simple discharge has been obtained. It obviously makes a difference to the lending world that a guy made the effort to see it through, even when things were bad, rather than just pulling the chain and flushing his creditors.

I finish this chapter where I started, encouraging all who might find themselves contemplating pursuing this course to move cautiously and thoughtfully—even prayerfully—before taking this direction. If things are bad enough that you think this is an answer, it's probably true that your credit rating already looks awful, so there's not necessarily a lot to lose by trying other alternatives first. The yellow pages contain the names of numerous good credit counseling services, and they deserve your attention before giving up. It's even possible to get your bank to help, especially if they hold your mortgage and have a stake in your success. A second job, liquidation of some nonessential items, or a loan from family to put out the worst fires are ideas that can help get you out of the mess you're in. And if bankruptcy or liquidation is in fact the final answer, hire someone good and do it right. There can be no worse result than going through all this, only to discover that some creditor who was a real problem was skipped or a lien on your house was still in place after the whole thing was finished. But most of all change the ways that got you there. Resolve to avoid the things that created this mess, and do all you can to be a better steward of your family's money.

CHAPTER EIGHT
⚖ Wills and Probate

THE GENERAL PUBLIC IS PROBABLY MORE UNCOMFORTABLE AND LESS IN formed about this subject than any area of the law. People view it as a combination of voodoo, greed, graft, corruption and black magic, with just enough of the IRS thrown in to scare everyone involved into hiding under the bed, and sadly, with just cause. At least the history of the area could lead one to such conclusions. Over the two centuries of American jurisprudence, this area has undergone huge changes, but most of them have been recent, as big attorneys' fees, high taxes on modest estates, and long, expensive proceedings were the rule until late in the last century.

However, today things are drastically different than they were even thirty years ago when I first started working in the area as a student clerk. Most folks have no exposure to federal estate tax these days, as the exemptions and minimum estate size have gone up significantly, and attorneys' fees are now strictly controlled by the court and based upon the hours worked, not a percentage of the estate involved. And although this may not be true in cases of unsupervised administration, if the heirs complain and the courts get involved, this will still hold true there as well. Moreover, things like state inheritance taxes and "court costs"—that unknown evil everyone fears but doesn't understand—are typically of almost no concern in the average probate estate in Indiana today. There are even provisions in the probate law now that permit inexpensive, quick and efficient unsupervised administration of estates where certain conditions are met, and no administration is required *at all* on small estates where minimum dollar ammounts are not exceeded.

The Necessity of Wills

The subject of wills and will writing has always been a black hole for most folks, and even today the number of folks without one would surprise you. Unfortunately there has been a growing problem in the United States in recent years, as crooks and shysters have preyed on the fears and ignorance of older Americans, selling them on expensive estate plans and complicated wills when they needed neither. But with that said, let's be clear on one thing: **almost all adults should have a will.** Here is what they do for you and why it is important:

1. They eliminate some questions and arguments that can arise much more easily than one might imagine over items of property that at times might seem unimportant during your life.

2. They permit uneven distribution of an estate between heirs; this one helps the testator (the person who is disposing of his or her property by will) to protect improvident kids or spouses from themselves. Sadly not all kids are created equal in the money-handling department, and the mechanisms we use in will writing help guard against reckless or even just unwise spending.

3. Folks who have been married more than once, have a "his and hers" situation with kids of one who are not kids of the other, can devise ways to provide for all without sharing the estates or creating difficulties later. Some of this can get complicated, and the only answer here is good draftsmanship. That means a good will writer, someone who has done it before and has the patience and experience to tailor the document to the needs of the client.

4. Disinheritance. This one seems nasty, but the truth is, there's really only one good way to disinherit a person who would inherit by law unless a will were written, and that way is to do so in a will.

5. Providing for a young family is serious business and requires a will with trust provisions in it. Remember that when you die leaving minor children, unless the other parent of those kids is still alive, a guardian will have to be appointed to care for them and the property they inherit from you. And while Aunt Sally may be the best person in the world to raise the children, she may not have the skills and sophistication needed to handle the proceeds from hefty life insurance policies, your pension payments, or the proceeds from the sale of the family residence. So unless you want a court to make all those appointments *and all those decisions* for you, best write it down and do so correctly. We use trust provisions that are right in the will and that can be applied to life insurance proceeds simply by coordinating them with the insurance company. We can provide for a trustee named in the will to collect all assets and use them for the benefit of all the kids as you direct in that portion of the instrument.

6. Because wills only "speak" upon the death of the testator, they can be written in ways that grow with the estate. By making percentage distributions of property and naming a trusted person as personal representative, the estate that was small when the will was written can be well administered later even if it has grown much larger by the date of death.

7. They are also easily changed, amended (that's called a codicil) or revoked and completely rewritten during your life, whenever and wherever you choose. All that has to be done is for the changes or rewrites to be executed according to the statute as the original was.

8. It's the, only way to be sure you have provided for certain dire situations like the simultaneous death of both parents of minor children. The last thing anybody wants when something that awful has happened is for there to be conflict or indecision over what to do with the kids and who should do it. A copy of your will in the hands of that

person will remove all doubt and permit at least one feature of such a time to be smooth and without argument.

9. Wills with tax provisions in them or referred to in them for incorporation into an estate plan are the only way to minimize the huge bite that federal estate taxes can have on the property of the decedent. We won't talk in detail about that subject, as it is solely the business of the tax and estate-planning lawyer, but be advised that, if your estate meets certain minimum values, you cannot dodge the taxman without help, and I mean sophisticated, skilled help.

10. Unless you have a will, it is impossible to leave your property to anyone but your family. Those who die "intestate" have their property distributed by the statutes that provide for intestate succession, and those rules make no provision for your best friend, your cousin (unless he's all that's left when you die) your church or other charity, or your mate of long-standing whom you never got around to marrying.

PROBATE WITH INFORMAL AND UNSUPERVISED ADMINISTRATION

Not all estates are required to go through the process of formal administration. Estates where the net values do not exceed $25,000 may be disposed of with court approval on a "certificate of no administration" that simply permits the heirs to divide property as the will directs, by agreement and after execution of proper affidavits, so long as they wait at least ninety days from the date of the testator's death. The lawyer for the estate prepares a request to the probate court for authority to accomplish the provisions of the will, it gets spread of record, and after that required waiting period, everything gets done. The costs are modest, the lawyer gets paid an hourly fee, the taxes get paid, and the whole thing is finished.

Even if the estate is very large, a family can get through probate of a decedent's will with unsupervised administration, so long as everyone agrees, there are no fights, a bond can be posted, and the court approves the arrangement. This concept made a huge difference in the business of handling decedents' estates in Indiana, and in addition to speeding things up it resulted in a big decrease in cost and added other efficiencies as well. Often folks just go to the lawyer who wrote the will and get things going right there. There are numerous details that have to be remembered and attended to, and these folks are the ones who know what they are and how to handle them. These are some of those details.

1. The banks will freeze bank accounts, other than those that are joint with a surviving spouse. They pay attention to the death notices in the paper and are remarkably good at discovering when one of their customers has died. The only way to "unfreeze" the accounts is for someone to file with the Inheritance Tax Division of the Department of Revenue a request for a Consent to Transfer property of the decedent. And so long as it is clear to the inheritance tax folks that their interest in the estate is protected, they will issue the request immediately. But it has to be done, and without it, the money cannot be moved.

2. Access to a lock box is impossible without permission of the Inheritance Tax Division, and its appraiser *must be present when the box is opened.* This one can be sticky if the will is in there. Probate cannot be commenced without the original will, meaning a will with original signatures on it. Photostatic copies are not permitted for admission to probate. Obviously there are more people dying than there are tax appraisers, so it can take weeks to get into the box. The only way to get that process started is to make those arrangements among the appraiser, the bank, and the lawyer.

3. Death being the unpredictable element that it is, it often interrupts proceedings or arrangements right in the

middle of the word "if." Where the decedent was involved in the sale of property or a business, completing the transaction without him can be difficult. The law calls these "executory contracts," a phrase so peculiar to the law that it doesn't even appear in most general dictionaries. The court has to approve completion of the transaction, and the personal representative cannot act at all until the court appoints that person, he or she is adequately bonded, and arrangements can be made for him or her to finish the work the testator had started. And unless the lawyer can react quickly, sales can be lost or other opportunities missed in such situations.

4. When a person dies, a number of income and related tax consequences can flow from that event. That person's taxable year ends with death, so there is a federal and a state return to be prepared and filed. There is a form of income that the IRS calls "income in respect of a decedent" that is basically income earned during life but not paid as of the date of death. How that income is reported, when, and on what return can make a big difference on the tax bite that the estate will experience when it is declared and paid. All this has to be collected and decisions made—often with the assistance of the accountants—and there can be some important deadlines associated with those actions.

5. The death of a business owner can really make things difficult, especially when he or she was a signatory on a business account. Depending on how the business was held, the account may be frozen, leading to such problems as bounced payroll checks, late tax account transfers, and missed insurance premium payments for employee benefits. You will need to contact the Inheritance Tax Division to unfreeze any accounts.

6. Not everyone reacts with equal good sense at such time, and not everyone has the best interests of the estate in

mind. Immediate steps have to be taken to protect cash, valuables, and business assets where there is no one close to do so properly. If a parent dies without leaving a surviving spouse and the kids live far away, securing the property of the decedent, including the residence, accounts, vehicles, and the like is an instant requirement. Unfortunately such things can grow legs and walk away unless proper actions are taken. We once had a "friend" of an elderly decedent who decided he would just take over and "look after" the lady's stuff. Problem was, there was more taking going on than "looking after," so it was necessary to file an Intermeddling Petition, a request for the court to take emergency action to stop people from removing property by appointing someone to immediately take lawful possession of the decedent's property until the personal representative could be located. Where someone has been caring for a decedent prior to death, this kind of problem is much more likely to occur, and we have always stressed to our clients that such folks should not be permitted to have access to valuables, accounts, motor vehicles, or real estate without proper supervision and accountability. At death, there needs to be some method of denying access to all assets for all but the personal representative at once.

7. Life insurance proceeds may provide the only funds for funeral arrangements and other final expenses, and whether or not there will be an estate opened for the decedent, someone with authority from the decedent needs to make proper application for payment of those policies. What to do with the money should be no problem, as the named beneficiaries will get the payment, but if payment is to be made to the estate, there is no choice but to open one for that purpose. Often, if a surviving relative has the resources to do so, funeral arrangements can be paid for, then they can be reimbursed by the estate after these payments have been received.

Will Requirements and Placement

To be effective under the laws of Indiana, a will must be witnessed by two people, and they must observe the testator signing the instrument. They must also then sign it as witnesses *in the presence of the testator and of each other.* There is a standard "self-proving" affidavit that is attached to the will, making its entry into probate easier, and we have always required the testator and witnesses to execute every page of the document. There is no reason to go cheap here, attempting to do this one yourself. Wills are not expensive when drafted by the lawyer, and the lawyer's office staff will then supervise the execution of the will.

Care for the completed documents is always a question. Many folks like to use their bank's safe deposit facilities for their important papers, but this is not necessarily the best answer. As I mentioned earlier, the state's inheritance tax appraiser must be present during all box openings, and that can take time. And because the estate cannot be opened and work begun on the matters we discussed above until that happens, having it more accessible is really a better idea. Ever since Gale Graber and Jim Sandifer broke me into this business thirty years ago, we have always maintained a will file in our offices, and most lawyers who do estate planning and estate probate do so as well. A small fireproof safe at home, big enough for insurance policies and will and trust documents is a good answer also, but it's important to make sure someone knows where that stuff is. We often make notes in our own files about the location of these items, so when family members call we can refer them to the right place.

Again, getting it right is imperative. And as unpleasant as it is for most of us to face our own mortality, getting these things cared for properly and with appropriate attention to the details we have addressed can be a huge gift to those you leave behind.

Death Taxes

One of the great fears and unknowns for those who must contemplate disposition of their assets upon death is that of the taxes that will be due when they die. In addition to income taxes that will become due at some point following death, there are two taxing authorities that may have claims against the estate: the state and the federal government. We will quickly dispose of the State of Indiana, as the state inheritance tax laws are of little consequence to most folks. Unlike federal estate taxes, the state inheritance tax is modest for most estates, and surviving spouses are exempt altogether. Folks further removed in relationship from the decedent are taxed on their portions of an estate, but the rates are pretty easy to handle. No one should spend much time fretting over what the state will take when Grandpa dies, but the same cannot be said for Uncle Sam.

Federal estate taxes are collected by the Internal Revenue Service, and they are complicated, severe, and painful. The good news is that the minimum size of an estate to be liable for these taxes has gone up in recent years, so that now, those who leave estates with a gross value of less than one million dollars pay no tax. There are also several deductible items that reduce the tax bite, and Congress has recently passed legislation that will eventually dispose of this one completely. But the rates are high, and for those who are exposed to them and have failed to do any tax planning, the feds can tax upwards of half the estate. I know it sounds immoral, but then we are talking about the IRS, so don't look there for fairness or morality. It would be impossible to try to describe the hoops you have to jump through to dodge some of this grief, but let me be clear. Anyone whose gross estate is likely to approach or exceed one million dollars, *including the value of all jointly held property and* **all life insurance proceeds,** needs to see a competent estate planning attorney without delay. We use things called "applicable credit amounts" or "applicable exclusion amounts" to avoid the specter of double taxation when the second spouse dies, and although these plans are not cheap, they are of huge importance in avoiding complete confiscation of the estate upon the second death of a married couple.

There is some tax planning that can include moving property around during the lifetime of the testator, and although there are limitations, one can give away a fair amount of property during life and avoid the tax consequences of both state and federal claims. For those who have substantial assets and meet certain criteria, trusts with generation-skipping features and other bells and whistles can also be of great significance. We will not go into the limitations on both, because they change as Congress and the legislature play with the tax laws.

CHAPTER NINE
⚖ Health Care

W E BEGIN THIS HUGELY IMPORTANT AREA OF THE LAW AND OF PEOPLE'S lives by warning our readers that this is the most complicated, confusing, constantly changing area discussed within these pages. Except for our old pals at the IRS, there is no other place that has so many tripwires, potholes, surprises, and unpredictable conclusions as the area of health law. Health care lawyers are frequently asked the following question, "Who will make medical decisions for me if I become incompetent?" Although there is a simple answer, you must be aware of how you may first encounter the question, in order to be best prepared to answer.

ADVANCE DIRECTIVES

In 1991 the federal government, in its most infamous wisdom, passed a law addressing "advance directives." The first problem encountered was that no one outside of a handful of lawyers and bureaucrats had any idea what the term "advance directive" meant. There are two basic kinds of advance directives. One is a document that is created by an individual to give direction to a health care provider as to how to proceed with treatment once the patient becomes incompetent. The other appoints a representative to make the incompetent patient's health care decisions in consultation with health care professionals. It's a somewhat contrived term. "Health care directive," would have been a better name for such a document. Most people would have understood what was being discussed if the term "health care directive" had been used to describe the concept.

Once we get a grip on what is meant by advance directives in general, we need to know how to create one. Each state has laws that describe how to create an advance directive, though the states do not refer to the documents by that name. The documents described in state laws are traditionally called living wills, appointments of health care representatives and powers of attorney for health care.

The second folly in the federal law is that a person is asked about his or her advance directive at a time when one is entering a hospital, nursing home, hospice, or health maintenance organization (i.e. managed care plan). This is an egregious error. There is no worse time for anyone to ask you what you have in place to direct your health care providers should you become terminally ill and or unable to make health care decisions. Folks entering a hospital are already anxious and considering the worst. Why rub it in? Further, in order to make such an important decision, we must have information about what legal and medical options are available. Of course the registrar at the hospital is totally unable to help a patient with any of this information.

Indiana law provides that certain persons are appointed by law to be your health care decision makers or "surrogates," in case you are permanently or temporarily incapacitated. If a person is married, that person's spouse is his or her health care representative, by law, unless a different person is appointed in writing or by a court. Since most people have only one spouse, this is a common and workable solution.

If an individual is unmarried but has adult children, those children are the health care decision makers. This can be problematic if the individual has more than one child and those children do not agree about health care treatment. If you suspect that your children will disagree about what kind of care you would want, or would argue with each other, you should decide who best knows your mind and wishes and appoint that child as your "health care representative," or power of attorney for health care.

If you have no spouse or adult children, competent parents should be appointed power of attorney. Again since this category potentially contains more than one individual, we need to consider whether to appoint one parent to make the decisions. The same is true of adult siblings, who would be next in line.

If for any reason an individual has a court appointed guardian, that guardian is automatically the health care representative. For those who are members of religious orders, the "superior" of that order is the individual's health care representative by law, unless another is appointed in writing.

Obviously then, if you are married and you want your spouse to make medical decisions for you should you become incompetent to do so, there is no need to execute a written appointment of a health care surrogate. If you do not want your spouse to make these decisions, execute a health care directive and take it with you every time you enter a hospital or other health care facility. Since this chapter is limited to legal advice, you are on your own as to how you will explain to your spouse why he or she will not be making any health care decisions about you. Better yet, wait until you are unaware of what is going on and let the hospital employees tell her or him!

Consider which health care directive best suits your situation. Many people are aware of living will documents. These are creatures of the probate statute and resemble a last will and testament. Unless you draft your own language, the gist of what is contained in a living will that is drafted by a lawyer or found in ready-made forms is as follows: *Should I become terminally ill, and the burdens of proposed treatments outweigh the benefits of same, I want those treatments withheld or withdrawn.* Unless otherwise specified, nutrition and hydration will be withdrawn as a result of this language because those are considered "health care," under Indiana law. Typically living will directives say that your physician is to be consulted with respect to these decisions.

What is wrong with the living will concept? First of all, it is pretty easy for your physician to avoid following your living will directive. Your physician can do this by simply refusing to conclude that you are "terminally" ill, because that term is loosely defined in Indiana law. Some consider "terminally" ill to be a projection that death will come in less than six months. Others believe that death must be much more imminent.

Then the family and medical team must wrestle with the idea

of whether the proposed treatment is a benefit or a burden. Will the treatment prolong life or extend an agonizing death? It is not always easy to determine that as medical science is far from exact and is sometimes not so very far from guess-work or hope. So much depends on the outlook of the people involved in such a decision. This stuff is no fun to deal with, but thinking these things through is best done now, not later.

At best a living will should be used in conjunction with an appointment of a health care representative. The result of dual documents is that in situations that are temporary and not life and death, the health care surrogate or representative can talk with the medical team, consider the facts at hand, and proceed. If the situation is terminal, the patient's wishes with respect to artificial life prolonging measures are known and can serve as guidance to the health care representative.

▶Power of Attorney for Health Care

A power of attorney for health care is similar to a power of attorney to conduct business for another. This power is limited in duration and function.

Often elderly people will appoint another as a power of attorney to conduct all business in case of incompetency. This power is expanded or limited by the contents of the documents. The power does not arise until the grantor becomes incompetent and ends when competency returns. The power dies with the grantor and does not continue postmortem. The most important point here is that the power of attorney cannot be used to make health care decisions unless it specifically says that the person appointed has that power. In other words, the person you appoint to conduct business during a period of incompetency is not your health care surrogate unless you specifically provide that assignment in the document.

Another important point of confusion about powers of attorney is that the person so appointed is NOT a guardian. **Individuals cannot appoint guardians.** Guardians are only appointed by a court of law. The confusion arises when one executes a form power of attorney. These forms usually say that the grantor desires that the person appointed as power of attorney be appointed as guardian. This statement does not have the effect of appointing a guardian. It is only meant to tell a court that the grantor prefers the person appointed as power of attorney to be his or her guardian should the need for a guardian arise.

Powers of attorney must be notarized. To create such a document is considered the practice of law, so should be done by an attorney. This requires considerable advance planning and will involve legal fees. Such is also the case with living wills. But again we say, the expense is not significant, the effort minimal on your part, and the resulting product very important. *Don't worry about the fees, as they are modest in almost all cases for work like this.*

Living wills are, as was previously stated, probate documents and must be executed just like a last will and testament—signed in the presence of two witnesses who sign as witnesses in the presence of one another. If a living will or power of attorney for health care is not prepared and signed as required by law, the document could be challenged and found invalid when the need for it arises.

Therefore, the best advance directive to use is a health care representative appointment. It is a short document, naming the individual who is to make health care decisions for a patient who becomes incompetent. It requires only one witness, does not need to be prepared by an attorney, and can be changed easily and as often as desired. If you want to appoint a health care representative, do so before you are admitted to a hospital, nursing home, or other facility. In addition to appointing a representative, you can add specific directions in this document—for instance, you can state that, "under no circumstances do I want a blood transfusion."

Regardless of which health care directive is used, discuss your medical wishes with your physician. Be sure you understand what you are "directing" in your health care directive. If you think you want only "comfort measures" and no "heroic medicine," do you understand the meaning of those terms? A young lawyer once called me from the hospital. He had wisely had his father execute an "advance directive" which appointed him as the health care representative and stated that his father wanted "only comfort measures" should he be admitted to the hospital. The son called me because he did not know what "comfort measures" were. I explained that a physician should be consulted but, in general, "comfort measures" are those merely intended to ameliorate pain for a patient whose disease or condition cannot be further treated or cured. They include pain medications, hydration (sometimes), and personal attention to bedding, surroundings, and visitation. Some individuals have stated that they did not want to be on a breathing machine. Be sure you understand the consequences of such a request. The language seems much clearer when there is no emergency or issue at hand, but when a real "life or death" decision is at hand, things can get pretty messy.

This is one of those times when my "get a lawyer" advice has to be secondary to checking things out with your doctor. Knowing the law in this area is not enough. You must talk to your physician about basic medical concepts you will be addressing in your document and talk to the person you have appointed to make health care decisions. Your health care surrogate must know you and your wishes and be willing to abide by those wishes. If not, the entire purpose of an advance directive for health care will be thwarted.

Mental Health Treatment

Society has always had trouble dealing with mental illness. In darker times we coped with those who were mentally ill by shutting them up in an asylum and/or filling them with tranquilizers. Compared to times when we used incarceration or excessive medication, we are "enlightened" in this area today. Mental illness has come to be recognized as a "disease like any other," as is the slogan of the National Alliance for the Mentally Ill. Treatment options range from outpatient therapy at home and partial hospitalization, to group homes and supervised apartment living. The trend is actually away from residential treatment. Drug therapy has benefited from much research and today's psychotropic drugs, antidepressants, and anxiety remedies have fewer side effects and are more effective.

We've also made huge progress in the quality of life now possible for those suffering from a mental illness. However, other problems continue to arise when mentally ill people are being treated within society rather than locked away from it. Stabilization of the disease is often temporary and de-compensation can occur at any time. Patients stop taking medication for various reasons and symptoms recur. A family member with a mental illness is living at home and working regularly one week, and out of control the next. What do we do in that instance?

The purpose of this section is to give general guidance and explain how the legal system may be used to assist families when mental illness causes a major disruption. Indiana has extensive legal procedures for seeing that those who need mental health treatment get it, and Indiana's involuntary commitment statute has several methods for helping families or friends get treatment for mental illness when necessary. They are voluntary commitment, immediate detention, emergency detention, involuntary regular commitment, and involuntary temporary commitment. But WARNING—these procedures are specific, at times very complicated, and often imprecise at best. We recently had a case with a sick adolescent that took us months to straighten out, with the presence of a divorce in the middle of the whole mess only making things worse. After trying to get his father to help (the guy disappeared like smoke when it became clear that his son was really sick) we went through every possible solution before Mom finally had to bite the bullet and put him in private care. We'll set out some of the problems and potential solutions by using a hypothetical situation; let's look at what these are and how they work.

Joseph was a twenty-eight-year-old male diagnosed with paranoid schizophrenia. His first episode occurred while he was in college and about twenty-one years of age. He flunked out of school even though he had previously maintained what had been a stellar GPA—3.8 on a 4.0 scale. He was pre-law. After one short and two longer hospitalizations, Joe went home to live with his mother. He was taking medications that had been successful in stabilizing his condition, he saw a therapist at the local community mental health center, and had a psychiatrist who monitored his medications. He even had a job at the local market and enjoyed his interaction with the customers.

Then his mother began to see his behavior deteriorate. He stayed in his room more and more. He was easily angered and irritated by the smallest things. He would not eat dinner with the family. Finally he began to talk incessantly about the neighbors and how they were spying on him and trying to hurt him. The situation escalated to the point that one night Joe locked himself in his room with a gun and said he would shoot anyone who entered. He felt he needed to protect himself against the neighbors who were going to capture him and turn him over to an alien government. Well, Mom was scared to death but decided not to call the police because she knew Joe was mentally ill and was afraid he would get himself shot in an altercation with them. When Joe started randomly throwing furniture out his bedroom window at the neighbor's house, someone there called the police.

When the police arrived, Joe's mother explained his mental illness and history. Fortunately the policeman on the scene had dealt with these situations before. He calmly talked Joe into opening the door. Joe was seized, handcuffed and taken to a local mental health hospital unit under an "immediate detention." The law gives the police the right to secure an individual and place him under twenty-four-hour detention to determine if he is mentally ill. If it cannot be determined in that first twenty-four-hour period, the facility holding the patient may file for an "emergency" detention, requesting that the person be held for seventy-two hours more in order to complete a mental health examination. This seventy-two-hour hold excludes weekends and holidays. Hence a person can be held for mental examination for twenty-four, seventy-two, ninety-six hours or more if weekends or holidays intervene. It's important to know that during this time the individual can accept treatment voluntarily, so if the patient decides to play ball, everything gets easier. However, if the patient is dangerous to himself or others, restraints or medications can be given on an emergency basis, without the patient's consent, in order to keep the patient or others safe. If during this detention period a patient is dangerous and/or gravely disabled and cannot be stabilized and refuses to voluntarily cooperate with treatment, a physician who examines the patient can report that to the proper court.

The physician's statement must establish that the patient is mentally ill as defined by Indiana law (this includes psychotic illnesses, depression, and other recognized mental illness as well as alcoholism, mental disability, and addictions) AND that the person is dangerous to himself or others and/or gravely disabled. *Grave disability means that the person lacks the judgment or ability to provide the daily necessities of life—food, clothing, and shelter.* It is often used when a person's delusions keep him from working, eating, or securing a home, even though the person is not dangerous to others or himself, except indirectly. Any patient would eventually suffer from malnutrition, exposure, or dehydration if the necessities of life were ignored. We had several cases where patients who were living successfully outside of any facility suddenly stopped taking their medications and really went downhill quickly. One woman stopped eating, turned the heat up to ninety degrees in her apartment (this was in July) and refused to let anyone into her apartment to help her. Another guy disappeared for several days, only to be discovered sleeping under a bridge, without a coat or other protection, in January.

If the physician requests an involuntary commitment hearing, the patient will be given notice of it and the process will continue to court, where the judge will determine whether, by clear and convincing evidence, the patient is mentally ill and/or dangerous to himself or others. If that person is found to meet the criteria for involuntary commitment, he or she will be ordered to inpatient or outpatient therapy as determined by his physicians. The commitment may be for a period of less than ninety days—a temporary commitment—or more than ninety days—a regular commitment. A regular commitment is for one year and can be extended for additional one-year periods upon recommendation of the patient's physician or the superintendent of the facility in which he or she is being treated. Indiana law provides processes that permit the patient to challenge the commitment to protect against any abuse of power. It's not hard to imagine just how abusive such a commitment might be for folks who are just more of an inconvenience to their families than real threats to themselves or others, so having a way to institute such a challenge is very important. And those who can't afford counsel can get public defender representation in many cases.

Clearly, calling the police to come to pick up a family member or friend is to be avoided at all costs. In certain circumstances like the one described, it cannot be helped. However, if Joe's family had known how to proceed and had intervened earlier, that trauma could have been avoided. What could they have done?

As we stated, his mother saw the beginning of Joe's deterioration. Joe was seeing a counselor at the community mental health center. Joe's mother should have consulted with the counselor and described what was happening at home. When Joe went in for an appointment, the counselor could have had him transported to the psychiatric unit of the hospital for an evaluation. Another option would have been for Joe's mother to drive him to the hospital instead of to his outpatient appointment. At the hospital he could have been retained and stabilized.

If Joe's condition could not be stabilized within the seventy-two hours the hospital had if it applied for emergency detention, the hospital superintendent or Joe's attending physician could have requested an involuntary commitment hearing. At the hearing Joe would have been represented by an attorney of his choice. If Joe could not afford an attorney, a public defender, well versed in the rights and circumstances of mental health commitments, would have represented him. He could have witnesses for him and would be entitled to cross-examine those who testified against him. All due process rights would have been afforded him. If he had been committed, he would have had the right to have his commitment reviewed once per year as a matter of right and more often for cause.

What if Joe had left the family home and family members could not have taken him to a mental health facility for treatment or transfer? Indiana law provides that a family member who observes the patient's dangerous or gravely disabled behavior can go to a court with mental health jurisdiction. There that family member could testify as to the circumstances that form a reasonable belief that Joe is mentally ill and dangerous to himself or others or is gravely disabled. If the court agrees, the court will issue a warrant to local law enforcement to pick Joe up and take him to an appropriate facility for determination of his mental status. The process described above begins at that point. If Joe is examined and found to be mentally stable, he will be released.

If he is dangerous to himself or others, gravely disabled, and/ or mentally ill he will be detained and may voluntarily agree to treatment. If he does not agree to medically necessary treatment for his mental illness, his doctors will ask for a commitment hearing as previously described.

Things do not always proceed as well as with our hypothetical patient, Joe. It may be that the individual in question is not sufficiently dangerous to himself or others or gravely disabled enough to warrant court intervention. He may not have a mental condition that is recognized by the courts as a "mental illness." Unfortunately many people who fall short of the criteria used to determine that mental health treatment should be rendered are instead sent to jail. It is also common for people who are mentally ill to be arrested and prosecuted for crimes that were either committed without sufficient understanding of the reality of the situation or committed with no intent to violate the law at all. Several Indiana counties have programs called "Pair." If an individual fits the profile of one who is mentally ill, he will be examined by a mental health counselor. If it is determined that the defendant is mentally ill, and the crime is a misdemeanor or minor crime, the individual will be diverted to the mental health system for commitment and treatment.

If your family member or loved one is mentally ill and in jail, inquire whether there has been a mental health examination and determination. You may encounter unenlightened individuals who protest saying, "everyone says they were out of their mind when the crime occurred." If you are sure of the mental illness, press the matter. Bring mental health records to the prosecutor or the individual's public defender to show that this is a legitimate case of mental illness and not a criminal act. Call the local mental health association or nearest chapter of the National Alliance for the Mentally Ill (NAMI) for guidance and assistance.

The purpose of this section is to make you aware of the issues. You need to know how to begin. You also need to know what questions to ask. If you find yourself in one of those situations, it is important to explore community resources for the mentally ill and to make use of what is available to you. Most people are not hardened to the plight of the mentally ill, but they simply do not understand the situation or the illness that is causing the problems. Fear and misunderstanding breeds the unwillingness to help. Each of you must serve as a teacher if our communities are to better serve the mentally ill population.

Medicare

Medicare is a federal insurance policy primarily for United States senior citizens. It is not an entitlement program. Most everyone has paid money through social security deductions, as premiums of a sort, for eventual Medicare benefits. If you do not qualify for benefits because you have had insufficient payroll deductions as a working adult, you will be able to receive maximum Medicare benefits. However, you must pay premiums just like you would for any other health insurance policy. Medicare is divided into two "parts." Medicare Part A covers primarily inpatient services such as hospital admissions and nursing home care. Medicare Part B covers "suppliers." This includes physician services, medical devices, outpatient care, and much more. This whole area is complex and most confusing, but it is important that we at least make you aware of the basics of coverage and the issues that sometime relate to things that are *not* covered.

▶ Eligibility for Medicare

Most commonly, a person who is eligible for Social Security becomes eligible for Medicare benefits at age sixty-five. Under a special transitional provision, some individuals who have reached age sixty-five, but have not met other eligibility requirements, are "grandfathered" into the program. Permanent residents who have resided in the U.S. for five years and U.S. citizens who have attained the age of eligibility, but are not otherwise entitled to Medicare benefits, may enroll in the Part A program if they pay a monthly premium.

Disabled individuals who have been entitled to disability benefits for at least twenty-five consecutive months under the Social

Security or Railroad Retirement programs are eligible for Medicare benefits. Folks with end-stage renal disease (ESRD) are eligible for Medicare benefits after a three-month waiting period, with certain exceptions including transplant recipients and self-dialysis trainees.

▶Medicare Services

Inpatient hospital care coverage includes costs of semi-private rooms, meals, regular nursing services, operating and recovery room, intensive care, inpatient prescription drugs, laboratory tests, x-rays, psychiatric hospital services, inpatient rehabilitation, and long-term care hospitalization when medically necessary, as well as all other medically necessary services and supplies provided in the hospital. Part A coverage is available for each day of inpatient hospital care, up to a maximum of ninety days per "spell of illness." However, from the sixty-first through the ninetieth days of hospitalization a deductible and a coinsurance charge reduce coverage.

Part A coverage is available for each day of extended care or skilled nursing services up to a maximum of one hundred days per "spell of illness." A beneficiary must have been an inpatient of a hospital for at least three consecutive calendar days and have been transferred to a participating Skilled Nursing Facility—SNF—usually within thirty days after discharge from the hospital. Such services must also be certified (and re-certified) as "medically necessary" by a physician, nurse practitioner, or clinical nurse at the time of admission or as soon thereafter as is reasonable and practicable.

Home health care services include care that is provided by a home health aide, or care that is furnished part-time by a home health agency in the residence of a homebound beneficiary. Certain medical supplies and durable medical equipment (DME) may also be provided. Certification (and re-certification) by a physician is necessary. Federal law provides that, after 1998, most home health care spending is being transferred to Medicare Part B.

Hospice care is a service provided to those terminally ill persons with a life expectancy of six months or less who elect to forgo the standard Medicare treatment benefits and receive only hospice care. Such care includes pain relief, supportive medical and social services, physical therapy, nursing services, and symptom management for a terminal illness

▶ *Medicare Providers*

"Conditions of participation" are used by the Secretary of Health and Human Services (HHS) to determine a provider's eligibility to participate in the Medicare and Medicaid programs. Providers who wish to accept assignment from Medicare beneficiaries must pass and continue to meet strict criteria in order to be certified as a Medicare provider. If you expect the provider you choose to accept your Medicare benefits as payment in full for your care (less deductible, co-pay or non-covered services), you should ask whether that provider is Medicare certified and "accepts Medicare assignment." You may go to a "non-participating" provider (one who is either not Medicare certified or does not accept Medicare in full as described above), but you will have to file your own Medicare claim and pay the provider in full. In that case, Medicare will not pay the full charge of a non-participating provider. **Medicare always pays less than a provider's charges.**

Medicare does not pay for all services you may need, and it does not pay for outpatient drug prescriptions. Therefore you will need what is called, "Medi-gap," or supplemental health insurance. Many insurance companies offer this supplemental insurance; AARP, the American Association of Retired Persons, has entered into contracts with such insurance carriers in order to obtain group prices for these policies. Do some shopping around to find the best deal for a supplemental health insurance policy when you become a Medicare recipient.

▶ *Payment System*

Understanding how Medicare providers are paid can help you understand what is happening to you when you are discharged from the hospital in record time, or have about five seconds with your doctor these days instead of the forty-five minutes you had in the "old days."

Hospitals are paid for inpatient services to Medicare beneficiaries on the basis of diagnostic related groups (DRGs) which are established at discharge. The DRG system classifies diseases by diagnosis and assigns patients to one of twenty-five major diagnostic categories. Costs included in the Prospective Payment System (PPS) rate are: inpatient operating, routine ancillary care such as nursing, intensive care, malpractice insurance, and pre-admission services. Costs excluded from the PPS rate are: direct medical education, heart, kidney, liver and lung acquisition, non-physician anesthetists, other non-physician professional costs, outpatient services, services covered under Medicare Part B, and all non-covered services. Certain pre-admission non-physician outpatient services furnished by the hospital or a facility owned or operated by the hospital, such as radiology or laboratory services, are included billable as separate services if furnished within seventy-two hours of the patient's admission.

It's pretty obvious at this point that the shorter your hospital stay, the more money the hospital makes. There is also great motivation for patients to receive fewer services.

As stated earlier, Medicare Part B includes payment for services of medical doctors (MD's) and doctors of osteopathic medicine (DO's). The following are also Part B providers, usually when their services are rendered outside an inpatient setting:

1. Limited license practitioners—dentists, oral and maxillofacial surgeons; optometrists; podiatrists; and chiropractors

2. Non-physician Clinical and Technical Personnel within certain parameters

3. Physical Therapists, Occupatal Therapists, and Speech Pathologists.

4. Clinical Psychologists and Licensed Clinical Social Workers

5. Certified Nurse Midwives

6. Certified Registered Nurse Anesthetists

7. Physician Assistants

8. Nurse Practitioners and Clinical Nurse Specialists

9. Audiology services

10. Diagnostic tests

11. Outpatient Providers and Freestanding Supplier Entities

12. Clinical laboratories

13. Comprehensive Outpatient Rehabilitation Facilities

14. Providers of outpatient Physical Therapy; Occupational Therapy, and Speech Pathology

15. Renal Dialysis Facilities

16. Federally Qualified Health Centers

17. Rural Health Clinics

18. Suppliers of Portable X-Ray Services

19. Ambulatory Surgical Centers

20. Outpatient services in Hospitals

21. Home Health Agencies

22. Medical Groups, Physician Professional Corporations, Physician Partnerships

23. Freestanding Radiation Therapy Centers

24. Sleep Disorder Clinics

25. Durable Medical Equipment, Prosthetics, Orthotics, and Supplies

26. Ambulance Services

27. Community Mental Health Centers

An individual is eligible to enroll for supplementary medical insurance (Part B) if he or she is entitled to Part A benefits. Anyone entitled to Part A coverage is automatically enrolled in Part B unless they decline coverage. To be eligible for Part B, a person must have attained age sixty-five and be a resident of the United States, or be an alien lawfully admitted for permanent residency, residing in the U.S. continuously during the five years immediately prior to enrollment.

Part B payment traditionally was based upon "reasonable charges," with the exception of certain certified suppliers and providers reimbursed on a reasonable *cost* basis. Effective January 1, 1992, the Health Care Finance Administration (HCFA) implemented a fee schedule payment methodology for physician and related practitioner services covered under Medicare Part B, replacing the reasonable charge payment mechanism for physician services with a national fee schedule. With the introduction of a fee schedule, your physicians, like the inpatient providers, made more money if they saw more patients during the course of a day. Since Medicare traditionally pays less than private insurance companies, there may be motivation to rush or hurry Medicare patients through treatment.

You may wonder why more often these days physicians prefer to do surgery in an ambulatory surgical center. Payment to the surgery center is based on a prospectively determined rate based on procedure. This rate covers the cost of services such as supplies, nursing services, equipment, and other related items. However, the rate does not cover physician services or other medical services such as X-ray services or laboratory services that are not directly related to the performance of the surgical procedures. Those services may be billed separately and paid on a reasonable charge basis. Often hospitals and physicians own the surgery centers because Medicare pays more per patient than what is paid either in a physician's office or when the same surgery is done in the hospital.

INDIANA MEDICAID

Medicaid is a cooperative program between federal and state government that is supposed to provide medical care to the indigent. Hence there are both federal and Indiana sources of the law.

Federal law sets certain minimum requirements that a state Medicaid program must follow, but federal law also gives a state certain options in deciding who to cover, what eligibility limits to set, and what medical services to provide. The Social Security Act established Medicaid. That law sets up requirements that a state Medicaid plan must meet.

Indiana law sets some eligibility requirements. The Indiana Family and Social Services Administration (IFSSA) is the agency which is ultimately responsible for the Medicaid program in Indiana. The Office of Medicaid Policy and Planning (OMPP), a division of IFSSA, is designated as the "single state agency" for administering Indiana's Medicaid program. OMPP is responsible for developing and coordinating Indiana's Medicaid policy, adopting administrative regulations, and administering the program at the state level, including such functions as paying claims and contracting with providers.

OMPP contracts with a private entity to perform various functions such as processing Medicaid payment claims, making prior approval determinations, and conducting level of care reviews at nursing homes.

►Eligibility for Medicaid

To qualify for Medicaid, certain financial guidelines must be met and a person must also fit within one of the covered groups. If the applicant does not fit within one of the covered groups, the applicant cannot receive Medicaid no matter how much he or she may need it. Most common is the disabled category. In addition there are welfare and "Aid to Families with Dependent Children" (AFDC) categories, which deal with the eligibility of persons such as pregnant women and children.

In order to be medically eligible for Medicaid, a person must be permanently disabled and unable to hold any kind of employment. This is a very high standard to meet. It is higher than the federal requirements that do not require a permanent disability.

Even if one meets the stringent medical criteria to qualify for Medicaid in Indiana, financial eligibility must also be met. Medicaid places limits on the amount of personal property a person eligible for Medicaid can have. There is no limit on the amount of real estate a person may have. However, if you own real estate other than your residence and are renting it out, the income earned from rent is counted toward income eligibility. If you own real estate that you are not renting out, you must offer it for rent or sale in order to qualify.

The limit on non-exempt personal property is $1,500 for a single person and $2,250 for a married couple. Only property that is available to the applicant/recipient is counted. Property is considered available if one "has a right, authority or ability to liquidate the property, or his share of the property."

Resources are valued on the first day of the month. Eligibility for a calendar month depends on the amount of the resources owned on the first day of the calendar month. This is actually interpreted to mean the first moment of the first day, so that income received on the first day or property disposed of on the first calendar day does not affect the resource calculation. There are exceptions to this "first day of the month rule." Direct deposit checks, like Social Security checks that are deposited on the first day of the month, are not counted. Checks written before the end of the month, but not cleared by the first day of the month are not counted.

Persons with excess resources below the Social Security Income (SSI) resource limits may be eligible for Medicaid. The SSI resource limits are $2,000 for a single person and $3,000.00 for a married person. Thus the applicant/recipient will be eligible but is responsible to pay for $500 of the medical expenses. This is called Medicaid "spend-down."

The following items are countable as resources when determining Medicaid financial eligibility:

1. Bank accounts

2. Stocks and Bonds

3. Life Insurance—cash surrender value

4. Cash

The following resources are not counted when determining Medicaid eligibility:

1. One motor vehicle if the applicant/recipient or a member of the household needs it for employment or for regular medical treatment, or if it is modified to transport or be operated by a handicapped person

2. Funds in reserve for burial and burial plots

3. Household goods

4. Proceeds from casualty insurance are exempt up to nine months if they are being used to repair or replace exempt property

5. Trusts—may be exempt or available. The rules are complicated and controversial, and as is clear from all this alphabet soup of regulations and bureaucracies, an attorney should be consulted

Lawyers well versed in this area will advise clients about planning for Medicaid eligibility. As you can see, placing all cash and other countable resources into one's home, care, pre-paid funeral plans, or household goods such as clothing, jewelry, or furniture will allow you to have many luxuries and still qualify for Medicaid.

There are special rules that allow for more exemptions for persons married to institutionalized persons. These rules let the person who is not in the institution keep more of the family's assets in order to continue to pay the cost of living. Medicaid will then pay for the nursing home care for the institutionalized spouse.

▶ Long-Term Life Insurance Program

In 1991 the Indiana legislature approved a law that allows for persons who purchase a qualified long-term care insurance policy approved by the Indiana Department of Insurance to protect their assets against use for medical care. For every dollar of benefits paid out under an individual's long-term care policy for Medicaid-eligible, long-term care services, that person's asset limit increases by the same amount.

For example, if Mom has a long-term care policy that pays $50.00 of nursing home care, her resource limit is $51,500.00 on the first day of the month. However, keep in mind the following:

1. The policy must meet the requirements listed in 760 IAC 2-20, the section of the Indiana Administrative Code that deals with all this

2. Policy must cover at least a year of nursing home care

3. Home and community care, as well as nursing home care, must be offered by the carrier, but the purchaser can choose to exclude it

4. Maximum policy benefits must be stated in dollars, not days

5. Daily nursing home benefits must be at least 75% of the average private pay rate

6. The policy must include information about inflation protection

7. Premiums must be based on the issue age of the policy-holder and cannot increase strictly due to the policyholder's advancing age

In addition to the resource limits there are income limits one must meet in order to be financially eligible for Medicaid. Current income limit is $494.00 per month for single people and $726 for married couples. These levels are adjusted annually to the SSI benefit levels. The income limit for a married couple is the same whether one or both spouses apply.

Some income is not counted:

1. $15.50 of an applicant or recipient's income is not counted

2. SSI benefits are disregarded

3. The first $65.00 of gross earnings are disregarded and then one-half of the remaining earnings are disregarded

The net income above deductions is referred to as "countable income."

Just like with resources, there is an income "spend down." If one's income is above Medicaid's current countable limits, but there are certain high medical bills, then he or she may be eligible for Medicaid to pay part of the medical expenses. Folks may be eligible for Medicaid after the income spend down requirements are met. For example, if your income is $594.00 per month, you are eligible for Medicaid after the first $100.00 of medical expense has been incurred that month.

Again as with resources, there are special rules for a single person in a nursing home and married people when both spouses are residing in a nursing home. This also applies to nursing home residents with spouses living at home (a "community spouse"). An attorney who concentrates in elder law, probate, or family law can assist with these "unique" rules.

At this point it might seem like a good idea to transfer your property to your children before you need Medicaid so that you will not have to spend all your assets to qualify. Nice try, but no cigar. People who transfer property for less than adequate consideration may be ineligible for Medicaid for a period of time. The transfer rules are federal, not state.

A transfer of property that results in a penalty period only makes the person ineligible for nursing home or certain long-term home care services. A person under a penalty can still receive Medicaid to pay their physicians, hospitals, pharmacists, and other providers for other Medicaid services.

A transfer of assets includes any cash, liquid assets, or property that is transferred, sold, given away, or otherwise disposed of as follows:

1. Converting an asset from individual to joint ownership

2. Relinquishing or limiting the applicant/recipient's right to liquidate or sell the asset

3. Disposing of a portion or a partial interest in the asset while retaining an interest

If an applicant/recipient relinquished ownership or control over a portion of an asset, but retains ownership, control, or an in-

FREE LEGAL ADVICE: INDIANA

terest in the remaining portion, the portion relinquished is considered transferred. Assets include income or resources of the individual or spouse.

Certain transfers are considered exempt.

1. There is no penalty for transfers to a spouse or disabled child, or to a trust for the "sole benefit" of the spouse or disabled child

2. There is no penalty for transfers of exempt property except for the home

3. The transfer of the home to a child under age twenty-one who was residing in the home for at least two years before the person becomes institutionalized and who provided care which allowed the person to live at home rather than in an institution is exempt from penalty

4. Transfers to a sibling with an equity interest in the home who resided in the home for at least one year before the person becomes institutionalized are exempt

5. Finally, no transfer penalty should be imposed if the applicant is able to satisfactorily show that the assets were transferred **exclusively** for a purpose other than to qualify for Medicaid. This is a very difficult standard to meet. One example that has been successful comes to mind. We had a client who transferred lake property to a son, but the client claimed it was not done to qualify for Medicaid. The family was able to show that the transfer of lake property to the son was not done to qualify for Medicaid, but was necessary because of the parents inability to maintain the lake home in their advanced ages. It worked in that case.

In determining a penalty for transfer, there is something called a "look back" date. This is the earliest time the Medicaid office will consider transfers as not violating the penalty provisions of the law. Transfers made before the look back date will never affect eligibility. The look back date is thirty-six months back from the first date when one is both in a nursing home and has applied for Medicaid.

The look back period for trusts is sixty months.

There is a formula for determining the length of any transfer penalty period. The penalty period is the period of months for which Medicaid will not cover certain expenses, such as the cost of nursing home care. It is as follows: **Amount transferred divided by the average cost of nursing home care equals months of penalty.** The months of penalty means the length of time Medicaid will not pay for nursing home care. For example, Dad transfers $50,000 total to his sons. Six months later Dad has to go a nursing home after suffering a stroke. The monthly cost of the nursing home is $2,500.00, which is the average cost of nursing home care in Dad's town.

Fifty thousand divided by twenty-five hundred equals twenty. The penalty period is twenty months, meaning that Medicaid will not pay for the first twenty months of his nursing home care.

▶Application Procedure

You apply for Medicaid at the County Office or at the Division of Family and Children. Any interested person can apply for the applicant—a spouse, other relative, friend, etc. The time limit for processing a Medicaid application is forty-five days, except that the time limit is ninety days if eligibility is sought based on disability.

If a Medicaid application is denied, the applicant may appeal the decision. Administrative appeals may be taken from any action or proposed action that is adverse to the applicant or recipient. Proposed actions to deny, suspend, or discontinue assistance are examples of the same. A recipient is entitled to receive ten days notice before any adverse action is taken. The notice must be mailed at least ten days before the effective date.

You do not need a lawyer to appeal. A fair hearing can be requested by any clear, written expression by the applicant/recipient, or representative requesting review or appeal. Reasons for hearing requests need not be included. The hearing request can be submitted to the County Medicaid Office or to the Division of Family and Children. Include a copy of the notice of adverse action. Appeals must be filed (received by the agency) within thirty days of the effective date. The appellant has the right to examine the entire case file, including any documents or records that the Division will use at the hearing. Fair hearings are presided over by an administrative law judge (ALJ) who is an employee of the Division who must not have been previously involved in the case. The appellant has a right to be represented by a lawyer or layperson. The Division will issue a Notice of Hearing approximately ten days to two weeks before the hearing.

The fair hearing decision must be issued within ninety days after the request for a hearing was made. If the losing party is dissatisfied with the hearing decision, a request may be made for a review by the designee of the Division. A request for review must be received by the Division within ten days following the receipt of the appeal decision by the appellant. This can be a simple letter. Additional evidence is not allowed. However, brief or written arguments may be submitted.

If the government still refuses to change its decision, Indiana law provides for judicial review of the agency decisions. At this point, it may be a good idea to engage an attorney because if the procedures are not followed, you could lose your right to proceed with the appeal. The petition must be filed within thirty days of the receipt of the Division's decision. The petition must be filed in the county circuit or superior court. It is in the nature of an appellant review of the agency record. No evidence may be submitted that is outside the record. The defendant is the Indiana Division of Family and Children. Each party to the proceeding must be served with a copy of the petition. A summons must be issued to the Director of the Division and the Indiana Attorney General.

Medicaid is a huge mess, made worse over the past decade by some inexplicable spending sprees on the part of our legislature and some of the poorest stewardship of public money you could imagine. The complexities we have seen are but a tiny example of the enormous black hole that is Medicaid in Indiana. It is the biggest single expenditure in our budget, and recent efforts to protect "the children" have resulted in an expansion of public medical assistance far beyond what any Hoosier would think was right in dealing with the poor. People who have the resources—*and the insur-*

ance—to care for their own kids now put them on Medicaid because the coverage is better and the treatments are FREE. Again I say, "only in America."

PROBLEMS WITH PRIVATE INSURANCE

Medicare and Medicaid affect specifically defined groups. Most of the population has private (non-governmental) health insurance through employers or a private policy for which a monthly premium is paid. Problems arise with health insurance when claims are not paid or your health care insurance carrier decides it will not cover the services rendered.

First of all, you need to understand that the contract of insurance is between you and your insurance company. If your insurance is through your employer, the employer has made all the decisions as to the kind of coverage to buy, what will be covered, and how much of each claim will be paid. You may not like it, but you are stuck with it.

When you go to the doctor and sign the release allowing the doctor to file your insurance claim, read the fine print. You are still required to pay everything your insurance does not pay. If your insurance pays nothing, you must pay the doctor's bill in full. You cannot pass this obligation to your doctor by saying, "Oh, that is covered by insurance." The physician's office is just doing you a favor by filing your claim. If the doctor is not promptly paid by your insurance, you will receive a bill that you are obligated to pay. You, the patient, must then fight with the insurance company to be repaid for services that are covered by your policy. Fortunately most physicians' offices will go to great lengths to get an insurance claim paid before turning to the patient for payment.

All this makes it very important for you to know what is covered by your health insurance. You must also know if there are limitations as to the providers you can go to for your health care. Many employers are buying an insurance product called "managed care." A typical managed care plan is a health maintenance organization (HMO) or a physician provider organization (PPO). If you are enrolled in an HMO or PPO, you must either go to a clinic owned and staffed by the HMO or to providers in the HMO network. The HMO has contracted with these network providers so that the HMO gets discounts in price in return for making sure patients go the providers who give the HMO the price breaks.

You should also know whether the health care you are seeking requires you to seek "prior authorization" or approval from your insurance carrier for a procedure. Again, most of the time your physician will see that this is done. The physician wants to be paid from the insurance company. However, you should check, because if the physician does not take care of this, you are responsible for the costs of care when the claim is denied for "lack of prior authorization." What about an emergency situation that arises suddenly at 2:00 a.m.? Insurance typically provides that you must notify the insurance carrier within forty-eight hours of the emergency service in order to secure coverage if the health care is on the list of services that require prior approval.

There is a Catch-22 with prior approval. Insurance carriers always put in a disclaimer that says that prior approval is not a "guaranty" of payment. The insurer reserves the right to change its mind later and deny payment for a service if it is later determined to be non-covered or medically unnecessary. You should know that not all these one-sided provisions in policies are enforceable, so if you get the feeling you've been hosed, it may be worth having counsel review the charges, the payments, and the treatment received before giving up.

Even if a physician and the service given are covered by your insurance, the service must have been "medically necessary." Here is where the insurance company gets the last word on whether it will pay. This is best shown by example. You have kidney stones. Your doctor orders a treatment called a lipotripsy whereby radiation blasts the stones into pieces that are easily and painlessly passed through urination. You found that, yes, lipotripsy is on the list of covered services in your plan and you are going to a provider who is on the plan list as well. You do not need prior approval for this procedure. After you are on your feet, you get a letter from your insurance carrier saying that the procedure is not covered for you because it was not "medically necessary." Why not? You had kidney stones and this is a perfectly acceptable treatment for some. However, the insurance company can maintain that lipotripsy was not medically necessary at this time. More conservative—or rather, "cheaper for them"—methods should have been tried first. That means that the physician should have let you try to pass that kidney stone while it was still whole.

Have you no rights? Yes, you have a few. Most insurance plans have appeal rights—ERISA rights. Some plans, such as employer self-funded plans, must give covered persons a chance to grieve or appeal adverse decisions because the law requires that they do. Many states have HMO or PPO "bill of rights" for patients, which give the patient rights to challenge bad decisions by the insurance carrier. In the case of plans covered by ERISA, the appeal rights and procedures should be on the back of the letter of "explanation of benefits" (EOB), which is the writing you received telling you the service is not medically necessary or covered. Check your insurance plan documents and exercise your rights. Do not hesitate as many appeals or grievances have limits. For instance you have sixty days to protest the decision. Most often you must submit your appeal in writing. Always keep a copy of everything the insurance company sends you and you send to the company.

This is just a small sample of the basics of dealing with private insurance. It is meant to make you think and to use whatever means of self-help are available to you to solve your problem. This area is highly regulated and you may find yourself in a situation you cannot handle. It is then time to seek professional help from your human resources department at work, your insurance agent, or an attorney. As was stated at the beginning of the book when we were addressing personal injury cases, there are just no "good hands" anymore. The insurance business has become ever so adversarial, even when the companies are dealing with their own insured customers. Having competent counsel is not just a good idea, it is an absolute requirement.

CONCLUSION

There you have it—all you never wanted to know about the law in the great State of Indiana. We end as we began, with encouragement that this intricate and at times maddening array of rights and responsibilities, duties and protections, have at their foundation the concept that we live in a society that is ordered and based upon the rule of law. I encourage you to review my admonitions contained in the introduction, and again I say, do not be afraid to seek counsel when the need arises. We enjoy such great freedom and have such a fine quality of life precisely because we have decided as a people that we will conform our behavior to established and well-defined rules. We also maintain that freedom by insisting, at every level of society, that our fellow citizens respect and follow those rules that our leaders have forged for us.

APPENDIX
Relevant Indiana Statutes and Forms

DOMESTIC RELATIONS

►*DIVORCE*

31-15-2-2
Sec.2. A cause of action for dissolution of marriage is established.

31-15-2-3
Sec.3. Dissolution of marriage shall be decreed upon a finding by a court of one (1) of the following grounds and no other ground:
 (1) Irretrievable breakdown of the marriage.
 (2) The conviction of either of the parties, subsequent to the marriage, of a felony.
 (3) Impotence, existing at the time of the marriage.
 (4) Incurable insanity of either party for a period of at least two (2) years.

31-15-2-8
Sec.8. Whenever a petition is filed, a copy of the petition, including a copy of a summons, shall be served upon the other party to the marriage in the same manner as service of summons in civil actions generally.

31-15-2-9
Sec.9. A responsive pleading or a counter petition may be filed under this chapter.

31-15-2-10
Sec.10. Except as provided in sections 13 and 14 of this chapter, in

an action for a dissolution of marriage under section 2 of this chapter, a final hearing shall be conducted not earlier than sixty (60) days after the filing of the petition.

31-15-2-11

Sec.11. If a petition has been filed in an action for legal separation under IC 31-15-3-2 (or IC 31-1-11.5-3(c) before its repeal), a final hearing on a petition or counter petition subsequently filed in an action for dissolution of marriage under section 2 of this chapter (or IC 31-1-11.5-3(a) before its repeal) may be held at any time after sixty (60) days after the petition in an action for legal separation under IC 31-15-3-2 has been filed.

31-15-2-12

Sec.12. (a) This section applies if a party who filed an action for dissolution of marriage under section 2 of this chapter (of IC 31-1-11.5-3(a) before its repeal) files a motion to dismiss the action.

(b) A party that files an action shall serve each other party to the action with a copy of the motion.

(c) A party to the action may file a counter petition under section 2 of this chapter not later than five (5) days after the filing of the motion to dismiss. If a party files a counter petition under this subsection, the court shall set the petition and counter petition for final hearing not earlier than sixty (60) days after the initial petition was filed.

31-15-2-13

Sec.13. At least sixty (60) days after a petition is filed in an action for dissolution of marriage under section 2 of this chapter, the court may enter a summary dissolution decree without holding a final hearing under this chapter if there have been filed with the court verified pleadings, signed by both parties, containing:

(1) a written waiver of final hearing; and

(2) either:

  (A) a statement that there are no contested issues in the action; or

  (B) a written agreement made in accordance with section 17 of this chapter that settles any contested issues between the parties.

31-15-2-14

Sec.14.(a) The court may bifurcate the issues in an action for dissolution of marriage filed under section 2 of this chapter (of IC 31-1-11.5-3 (a) before its repeal) to provide for a summary disposition of uncontested issues and a final hearing of contested issues. The court may enter a summary disposition order under this section upon the filing with the court of verified pleadings, signed by both parties, containing:

(1) a written waiver of a final hearing in the matter of :

(A) uncontested issues specified in the waiver; or

(B) contested issues specified in the waiver upon which the parties have reached an agreement;

(2) a written agreement made in accordance with section 17 of this chapter pertaining to contested issues settles by the parties; and

(3) a statement:

(A) specifying contested issues remaining between the parties; and

(B) requesting the court to order a final hearing as to contested issues to be held under this chapter.

(b) The court shall include in a summary disposition order entered under this section a date for a final hearing of contested issues.

31-15-2-15

Sec.15.(a) At the final hearing on a petition for dissolution of marriage the court shall consider evidence, including agreements and verified pleadings filed with the court. If the court finds that the material allegations of the petition are true, the court:

(1) shall enter a dissolution decree as provided in section 16 of this chapter; or

(2) if the court finds that there is a reasonable possibility of reconciliation, may continue the matter and order the parties to seek reconciliation through any available counseling.

(b) At any time forty-five (45) days after the date of a continuance:

(1) either party may move for the dissolution of the marriage; and

(2) the court may enter a dissolution decree as provided in section 16 of this chapter.

(c) If no motion for the dissolution is filed, the matter shall be, automatically and without further action by the court, dismissed after the expiration of ninety (90) days from the date of continuance.

31-15-2-16

Sec.16.(a) The court shall enter a dissolution decree:
 (1) when the court has made the findings required by section 15 of this chapter; or
 (2) upon the filing of pleadings under section 13 of this chapter. The decree may include orders as provided for in this article.

(b) A dissolution decree is final when entered, subject to the right of appeal.

(c) An appeal from the provisions of a dissolution decree that does not challenge the findings as to the dissolution of marriage does not delay the finality of the provision of the decree that dissolves the marriage, so that the parties may remarry pending appeal.

31-15-2-17

Sec.17.(a) To promote the amicable settlements of disputes that have arisen or may arise between the parties to a marriage attendant upon the dissolution of their marriage, the parties may agree in writing to provisions for:
 (1) the maintenance of either of the parties;
 (2) the disposition of any property owned by either or both of the parties; and
 (3) the custody and support of the children of the parties.

(b) In an action for dissolution of marriage:
 (1) the terms of the agreement, if approved by the court, shall be incorporated and merged into the decree and the parties shall be ordered to perform the terms; or
 (2) the court may make provisions for:
  (A) the disposition of property;
  (B) child support;
  (C) maintenance; and

(D) custody;

as provided in this title.

(c) The disposition of property settled by an agreement described in subsection (a) and incorporated and merged into the decree is not subject to subsequent modification by the court, except as the agreement prescribes or the parties subsequently consent.

31-15-2-18

Sec.18. A woman who desires the restoration of her maiden or previous married name must set out the name she desires to be restored to her in her petition for dissolution as part of the relief sought. The court shall grant the name change upon entering the decree of dissolution.

31-15-2-19, 20, 21, 23, 24 Repealed

▶*PROTECTIVE ORDERS IN DISSOLUTION AND LEGAL SEPARATION ACTIONS*

IC 31-15-51

Sec.1.(a) A party who obtains a temporary restraining order under IC 31-15-4-3(2) or IC 31-15-4-3(3) (or IC 31-1-11.5-7(b)(2) or IC 31-1-11.5-7(b)(3) before the repeal of IC 31-1-11.5-7) in a dissolution of marriage or legal separation action may request the court to issue a protective order for the same purposes set forth in the temporary restraining order:

(1) at the final hearing of the dissolution of marriage of legal separation action; or

(2) in the summary dissolution of marriage decree under IC 31-15-2-13.

(b) A party may request the issuance of a protective order under this section:

(1) at the final hearing of the dissolution of marriage or legal separation action;

(2) in the summary dissolution of marriage decree; or

(3) not later than sixty (60) days after the issuance of the final dissolution of marriage decree or legal separation decree.

As added by P.L.1-1997, SEC.7. Amended by P.L.197-1997, Sec.6.

IC 31-15-5-2

Sec.2. If:

(1) a party has not obtained a temporary restraining order or the factual basis or relief sought by the party in a temporary restraining order obtained by the party has changed; and

(2) the party requests a court to issue a protective order:

(A) at a final hearing of the dissolution of marriage or legal separation action;

(B) in a summary dissolution of marriage decree under IC 31-15-2-13; or

(C) not later than sixty (60) days after the issuance of the final dissolution of marriage decree or legal separation decree; the party must file an independent written , verified motion that established the factual basis or relief sought in the protection order.

As added by P.L.1-1997, SEC.7. Amended by P.L.197-1997, SEC.7.

IC 31-15-5-3

Sec.3. If the parties have an unemancipated child, a party may request the court to issue a protective order against the other party at any time after issuance of the final dissolution of marriage decree. To request the protective order, the party must file an independent written, verified motion that establishes the factual basis and the relief sought in the protective order.

As added by P.L.1-1997, SEC.7.

IC 31-15-5-4

Sec.4. A court may not require the moving party under this chapter to give security.

As added by P.L.1-1997, SEC.7.

IC 31-15-5-5

Sec.5. The court shall set a date for a hearing concerning a motion for an emergency protective order described in section 9 of this chapter not more than thirty (30) days after the date of the motion is filed with the court.

As added by P.L.1-1997, SEC.7.

IC 31-15-5-6
Sec.6. At the hearing, if at least one (1) of the allegations described in the motion is proved by a preponderance of the evidence, the court shall order the respondent to:
  (1) refrain from abusing, harassing, or disturbing the peace of the moving party, by either direct or indirect contact;
  (2) refrain from abusing, harassing, or disturbing the peace of a member of the moving party's household, by either direct or indirect contact;
  (3) refrain from entering:
    (A) the property of the moving party;
    (B) jointly owned or leased property of the moving party and the respondent if the respondent is not the sole owner or lessee; or
    (C) any other property; as specifically described in the motion;
  (4) refrain from damaging any property of the moving party; or
  (5) be evicted from the dwelling of the moving party if the respondent is not the sole owner or lessee of the moving party's dwelling.
As added by P.L.1-1997, SEC.7.

IC 31-15-5-7
Sec.7. The court may issue a protective order only upon showing of good cause.
As added by P.L.1-1997, SEC.7.

IC 31-15-5-8
Sec.8. A protective order under this chapter (or IC 31-1-11.5-8.2 before its repeal):
  (1) remains in effect for one (1) year; and
  (2) at the request of a party, may be renewed for not more than one (1) year.
As added by P.L.1-1997, SEC.7.

IC 31-15-5-9
Sec.9.(a) If a party requests the court to issue an emergency protective order, the court shall immediately review the motion ex parte. If the court finds that there is probable cause to believe that the

moving party, a member of the moving party's household, or the moving party's property was or is in danger of being abused or threatened with abuse by the respondent, the court shall:

(1) issue an emergency protective order directing the respondent to refrain from:

(A) abusing, harassing, or disturbing the peace of the moving party by either direct or indirect contact;

(B) abusing, harassing, or disturbing the peace of a member of the moving party's household, by either direct or indirect contact;

(C) entering the property of the moving party or any other property as specifically described in the motion; or

(D) damaging any property of the moving party; and

(2) set a date for the protective order hearing not more than thirty (30) days after the date the motion is filed with the court.

(b) An emergency protective order issued under this section (or IC 31-1-11.5-8.2(e) before its appeal) expires on the date a protective order hearing is held.

As added by P.L.1-1997, SEC.7.

IC 31-15-5-10

Sec.10. If a court issues a protective order under this chapter:

(1) the clerk of the court shall comply with IC 5-2-9; and

(2) the petitioner shall file a confidential form prescribed or approved by the division of state court administration with the clerk.

As added by P.L.1-1997, SEC.7.

►*ORDER FOR MAINTENANCE AND DIVISION OF PROPERTY*

31-15-7-1

Sec.1. The court may order maintenance in:

(1) final dissolution of marriage decrees entered under IC 31-15-2-16; and

(2) legal separation decrees entered under IC 31-15-3-9;

after making the findings required by section 2 of this chapter.

31-15-7-2

Sec.2. A court may make the following findings concerning maintenance:

(1) If the court finds a spouse to be physically or mentally incapacitated to the extent that the ability of the incapacitated spouse to support himself or herself is materially affected, the court may find that maintenance for the spouse is necessary during the period of incapacity, subject to further order of the court.

(2) If the court finds that:

(A) a spouse lacks sufficient property, including marital property apportioned to the spouse, to provide for the spouse's needs; and

(B) the spouse is the custodian of a child whose physical or mental incapacity requires the custodian to forgo employment;

the court may find that maintenance is necessary for the spouse in an amount and for a period of time that the court considers appropriate.

(3) After considering:

(A) the educational level of each spouse at the time of marriage and at the time the action is commenced;

(B) whether an interruption in the education, training, or employment of a spouse who is seeking maintenance occurred during the marriage as a result of homemaking or child care responsibilities, or both;

(C) the earning capacity of each spouse, including education background, training, employment skills, work experience, and length of presence in or absence from the job market; and

(D) the time and expense necessary to acquire sufficient education or training to enable the spouse who is seeking maintenance to find appropriate employment;

a court may find that rehabilitative maintenance for the spouse seeking maintenance is necessary in an amount and for a period of time that the court considers appropriate, but not to exceed three (3) years from the date of the final decree.

31-15-7-3
Sec.3. Provisions of an order with respect to maintenance ordered under section 1 of this chapter (of IC 31-1-11.5-9(c) before its repeal) may be modified or revoked. Except as proved in IC 31-16-8-2,

modification may be made only:

(1) upon a showing of changed circumstances so substantial and continuing as to make the terms unreasonable; or

(2) upon a showing that:

(A) a party has been ordered to pay an amount in child support that differs by more than twenty percent (20%) from the amount that would be ordered by applying the child support guidelines; and

(B) the order requested to be modified or revoked was issued at least twelve (12) months before the petition requesting modification was filed.

31-15-7-4

Sec.4.(a) In an action for dissolution of marriage under IC 31-15-2-2, the court shall divide the property of the parties, whether:

(1) owned by either spouse before the marriage;

(2) acquired by either spouse in his or her own right:

(A) after the marriage; and

(B) before final separation of the parties; or

(3) acquired by their joint efforts.

(b) The court shall divide the property in a just and reasonable manner by:

(1) division of the property in kind;

(2) setting the property or parts of the property over to one (1) of the spouses and requiring either spouse to pay an amount, either in gross or in installments, that is just and proper;

(3) ordering the sale of the property under such conditions as the court prescribes and dividing the proceeds of the sale; or

(4) ordering the distribution of benefits described in IC 31-9-2-98(b)(2) or IC 31-9-2-98(b)(3) that are payable after the dissolution of marriage, by setting aside to either of the parties a percentage of those payments either by assignment or in kind at the time of receipt.

31-15-7-5

Sec.5. The court shall presume that an equal division of the marital property between the parties is just and reasonable. However, this presumption may be rebutted by a party who presents relevant evidence, including evidence concerning the following factors, that an equal division would not be just and reasonable:

(1) The contribution of each spouse to the acquisition of the property, regardless of whether the contribution was income producing.

(2) The extent to which the property was acquired by each spouse:

(A) before the marriage; or

(B) through inheritance or gift.

(3) The economic circumstances of each spouse at the time the disposition of the property is to become effective, including the desirability of awarding the family residence or the right to dwell in the family residence for such periods as the court considers just to the spouse having custody of any children.

(4) The conduct of the parties during the marriage as related to the disposition or dissipation of their property.

(5) The earnings or earning ability of the parties as related to:

(A) a final division of property; and

(B) a final determination of the property rights of the parties.

31-15-7-6
Sec.6. If the court finds there is little or no marital property, the court may award either spouse a money judgment not limited to the property existing at the time of final separation. However, this award may be made only for the financial contribution of one (1) spouse toward tuition, books, and laboratory fees for the higher education of the other spouse.

31-15-7-7
Sec.7. The court, in determining what is just and reasonable in dividing property under this chapter, shall consider the tax consequences of the property disposition with respect to the present and future economic circumstances of each party.

31-15-7-8
Sec.8. Upon entering an order under this chapter, the court may provide for the security, bond, or other guarantee that is satisfactory to the court to secure the division of property.

31-15-7-9 Repealed
(Repealed by P.L.197-1997, SEC.29)

31-15-7-9.1
Sec.9.1.(a) The orders concerning property disposition entered under this chapter (or IC 31-1-11.5-9 before it repeal) may not be revoked or modified, except in case of fraud.

(b) If fraud is alleged, the fraud must be asserted not later than six (6) years after the order is entered.

31-15-7-10
Sec.10. Notwithstanding any other law, all orders and awards contained in a dissolution of marriage decree or legal separation decree may be enforced by:
  (1) contempt;
  (2) assignment of wages or other income; or
  (3) any other remedies available for the enforcement of a court order;
except as otherwise provided by this article.

▶*CHILD SUPPORT AND CUSTODY*

31-16-6-1
Sec.1. In an addition for dissolution of marriage under IC 31-15-2, legal separation under IC 31-15-3, or child support under IC 31-16-2, the court may order either parent or both parents to pay any amount reasonable for support of a child, without regard to marital misconduct, after considering all relevant factors, including:
  (1) the financial resources of the custodial parent;
  (2) the standard of living the child would have enjoyed if:
   (A) the marriage had not been dissolved; or
   (B) the separation had not been ordered;
  (3) the physical or mental condition of the child and the child's educational needs; and
  (4) the financial resources and needs of the noncustodial parent.

31-16-6-2

Sec.2.(a) The child support order or an educational support order may also include, where appropriate:

(1) amounts for the child's education in elementary and secondary schools and at institutions of higher learning, taking into account:

(A) the child's aptitude and ability;

(B) the child's reasonable ability to contribute to educational expenses through:

(i) work;

(ii) obtaining loans; and

(iii) obtaining other sources of financial aid reasonably available to the child and each parent; and

(C) the ability of each parent to meet these expenses;

(2) special medical, hospital, or dental expenses necessary to serve the best interests of the child; and

(3) fees mandated under Title IV-D of the federal Social Security Act (42 U.S.C. 651 through 669).

(b) If the court orders support for a child's educational expenses at an institution of higher learning under subsection (a), the court shall reduce other child support for that child that:

(1) is duplicated by the educational support order; and

(2) would otherwise be paid to the custodial parent.

31-16-6-3
Sec.3. As part of the child support order the court may set apart the part of the property of either parent or both parents that appears necessary and proper for the support of the child.

31-16-6-4
Sec.4. A child support order may also include, where appropriate, basic health and hospitalization insurance coverage for the child. If, however, the Title IV-D agency initiates action to establish a support obligation and petitions the court to include basic health and hospitalization insurance coverage in the support order, the court shall consider including a provision for insurance coverage for the child if the insurance coverage:

(1) is available to the parent ordered to pay child support or the

dependents of the parent as part of the parent's employee benefit plan; or

(2) is available at reasonable cost to the parent ordered to pay child support.

31-16-6-5

Sec.5. Upon entering an order under section 1 of this chapter, the court may provide for such security, bond, or other guarantee that is satisfactory to the court to secure the obligation to make child support payments.

31-16-6-6

Sec.6. (a) The duty to support a child under this chapter ceases when the child becomes twenty-one (21) years of age unless any of the following condition occurs:

(1) The child is emancipated before becoming twenty-one (21) years of age. In this case the child support, except for the educational needs outlined in section 2(a)(1) of this chapter, terminates at the time of emancipation, although an order for educational needs may continue in effect until further order of the court.

(2) The child is incapacitated. In this case the child support continues during the incapacity or until further order of the court.

(3) The child:

(A) is at least eighteen (18) years of age;

(B) has not attended a secondary or postsecondary school for the prior four (4) months and is not enrolled in a secondary or postsecondary school; and

(C) is capable of supporting himself or herself through employment. In this case the child support terminates upon the court's finding that the conditions prescribed in this subdivision exist. However, if the court finds that the condition set forth in clauses (A) through (C) are met but that the child is only partially supporting or is capable of only partially supporting himself or herself, the court may order that support be modified instead of terminated.

(b) For purposes of determining if a child is emancipated under subsection (a)(1), if the court finds that the child:

(1) has joined the United States armed services;

(2) has married; or

(3) is not under the care of control of :

(A) either parent; or

(B) an individual or agency approved by the court;

the court shall find the child emancipated and terminate the child support.

31-16-6-7

Sec.7.(a) Unless otherwise agreed in writing or expressly provided in the order, provisions for child support are terminated:

(1) by the emancipation of the child; but

(2) not by the death of the parent obligated to pay the child support.

(b) If the parent obligated to pay support dies, the amount of support may be modified or revoked to the extent just and appropriate under the circumstances on petition of representatives of the parent's estate.

IC 31-17-2-8

Sec.8. The court shall determine custody and enter a custody order in accordance with the best interests of the child. In determining the best interests of the child, there is no presumption favoring either parent. The court shall consider all relevant factors, including the following:

(1) The age and sex of the child.

(2) The wishes of the child's parent or parents.

(3) The wishes of the child, with more consideration given to the child's wishes if the child is at least fourteen (14) years of age.

(4) The interaction and interrelationship of the child with:

(A) the child's parent or parents;

(B) the child's sibling; and

(C) any other person who may significantly affect the child's best interests.

(5) The child's adjustment to the child's:

(A) home;

(B) school; and

(C) community.

(6) The mental and physical health of all individuals involved.

(7) Evidence of a pattern of domestic violence by either parent.

(8) Evidence that the child has been cared for by a de facto custodian, and if the evidence is sufficient, the court shall consider the factors described in section 8.5(b) of this chapter.

As added by P.L.1-1997, SEC.9. Amended by P.L.96-1999, SEC.7.

IC 31-17-2-8.5

Sec.8.5.(a) This section applies only if the court finds by clear and convincing evidence that the child has been cared for by a de facto custodian.

(b) In addition to the factors listed in section 8 of this chapter, the court shall consider the following factors in determining custody:

(1) The wishes of the child's de facto custodian.

(2) The extent to which the child has been cared for, nurtured, and supported by the de facto custodian.

(3) The intent of the child's parent in placing the child with the de facto custodian.

(4) The circumstances under which the child was allowed to remain in the custody of the de facto custodian, including whether the child was placed with the de facto custodian to allow the parent now seeking custody to:

(A) seek employment;

(B) work; or

(C) attend school.

(c) If a court determines that a child is in the custody of a de facto custodian, the court shall make the de facto custodian a party to the proceeding.

(d) The court shall award custody of the child to the child's de facto custodian if the court determines that it is in the best interests of the child.

(e) If the court awards custody of the child to the child's de facto custodian, the de facto custodian is considered to have legal custody of the child under Indiana law.

As added by P.L. 96-1999, SEC. 8.

IC 31-17-2-9

Sec.9.(a) The court may interview the child in chambers to ascertain the child's wishes.

(b) The court may permit counsel to be present at the interview. If the counsel is present:

(1) a record may be made of the interview; and

(2) the interview may be made part of the record for purposes of appeal.

As added by P.L. 1-1997, SEC. 9.

IC 31-17-2-10

Sec.10.(a) The court may seek the advice of professional personnel even if the professional personnel are not employed on a regular basis by the court. The advice shall be given in writing and made available by the court to counsel upon request.

(b) Counsel may call for cross-examination of any professional personnel consulted by the court.

As added by P.L. 1-1997, SEC. 9.

IC 31-17-2-11

Sec.11.(a) If, in a proceeding for custody or modification of custody under IC 31-15, this chapter, IC 31-17-4, IC 31-17-6, or IC 31-17-7, the court:

(1) requires supervision during the noncustodial parent's visitation privileges; or

(2) suspends the noncustodial parent's visitation privileges; the court shall enter a conditional order naming a temporary custodian for the child.

(b) A temporary custodian named by the court under this section receives temporary custody of a child upon the death of the child's custodial parent.

(c) Upon the death of a custodial parent, a temporary custodian named by a court under this section may petition the court having probate jurisdiction over the estate of the child's custodial parent for an order under IC 29-3-3-6 naming the temporary custodian as

the temporary guardian of the child.
As added by P.L. 1-1997, SEC. 9.

IC 31-17-2-12
Sec. 12. (a) In custody proceedings after evidence is submitted upon the petition, if a parent or the child's custodian so requests, the court may order an investigation and report concerning custodial arrangements for the child. The investigation and report may be made by any of the following:

(1) The court social service agency.

(2) The staff of the juvenile court.

(3) The local probation department or the county office of family and children.

(4) A private agency employed by the court for the purpose.

(5) A guardian ad litem or court appointed special advocate appointed for the child by the court under IC 31-17-6 (or IC 31-1-11.5-28 before its repeal).

(b) In preparing a report concerning a child, the investigator may consult any person who may have information about the child and the child's potential custodian arrangements. Upon order of the court, the investigator may refer the child to professional personnel for diagnosis. The investigator may consult with and obtain information from medical, psychiatric, or other expert persons who have served the child in the past without obtaining the consent of the parent or the child's custodian. However, the child's consent must be obtained if the child is of sufficient age and capable of forming rational and independent judgments. If the requirements of subsection (c) are fulfilled, the investigator's report:

(1) may be received in evidence at the hearing; and

(2) may not be excluded on the grounds that the report is hearsay or otherwise incompetent.

(c) The court shall mail the investigator's report to counsel and to any party not represented by counsel at least ten (10) days before the hearing. The investigator shall make the following available to counsel and to any party not represented by counsel:

(1) The investigator's file of underlying data and reports.

(2) Complete texts of diagnostic reports made to the investigator

under subsection (b).

(3) The names and addresses of all persons whom the investigator has consulted.

(d) Any party to the proceeding may call the investigator and any person whom the investigator has consulted for cross-examination. A party to the proceeding may not waive the party's right of cross-examination before the hearing.
As added by P.L. 1-1997, SEC. 9.

IC 31-17-2-13
Sec. 13. The court may award legal custody of a child jointly if the court finds that an award of joint legal custody would be in the best interest of the child.
As added by P.L. 1-1997, SEC. 9.

IC 31-17-2-14
Sec. 14. An award of joint legal custody under section 13 of this chapter does not require an equal division of physical custody of the child.
As added by P.L. 1-1997, SEC. 9.

IC 31-17-2-15
Sec. 15. In determining whether an award of joint legal custody under section 13 of this chapter would be in the best interest of the child, the court shall consider it a matter of primary, but not determinative, importance that the persons award joint custody have agreed to an award of join legal custody. The court shall also consider:

(1) the fitness and suitability of each of the persons awarded joint custody;

(2) whether the persons awarded joint custody are willing and able to communicate and cooperate in advancing the child's welfare;

(3) the wishes of the child, with more consideration given to the child's wishes if the child is at least fourteen (14) years of age; and

(4) whether the child has established a close and beneficial relationship with both of the persons awarded joint custody;

(5) whether the persons award joint custody:

(A) live in close proximity to each other; and

(B) plan to continue to do so.

(6) the nature of the physical and emotional environment in the home of each of the persons awarded joint custody.

As added by P.L.1-1997, SEC.9.

IC 31-17-2-16

Sec.16. Upon:

(1) the courts own motion;

(2) the motion of a party;

(3) the motion of the child; or

(4) the motion of the child's guardian ad litem;

the court may order the custodian or the joint custodians to obtain counseling for the child under such terms and conditions as the court considers appropriate.

As added by P.L.1-1997, SEC.9.

IC 31-17-2-17

Sec.17.(a) Except:

(1) as otherwise agreed by the parties in writing at the time of the custody order; and

(2) as provided in subsection (b);

the custodian may determine the child's upbringing, including the child's education, health care, and religious training.

(b) If the court finds after motion by a noncustodial parent that, in the absence of a specific limitation of the custodian's authority, the child's:

(1) physical health would be endangered; or

(2) emotional development would be significantly impaired;

the court may specifically limit the custodian's authority.

As added by P.L.1-1997, SEC.9.

IC 31-17-2-18

Sec.18. If both parents or all contestants agree to the order or if the court finds that, in the absence of the order, the child's physical health might be endangered or the child's emotional development significantly impaired, the court may order:

(1) the court social service agency;
(2) the staff of the juvenile court;
(3) the local probation department;
(4) the count office of family and children; or
(5) a private agency employed by the court for that purpose
to exercise continuing supervision over the case to assure that the custodial or visitation terms of the decree are carried out.
As added by P.L.1-1997, SEC.9.

IC 31-17-2-19
Sec.19. The court may tax as costs the payment of necessary travel and other expenses incurred by any person whose presence at the hearing the court considers necessary to determine the best interest of the child.
As added by P.L.1-1997, SEC.9.

IC 31-17-2-20
Sec.20. If the court finds it necessary to protect the child's welfare that the record of any interview, a report, or an investigation in a custody proceeding not be a public record, the court may make an appropriate order accordingly.
As added by P.L.1-1997, SEC.9.

IC 31-17-2-21
Sec.21.(a) The court may not modify a child custody order unless:
(1) the modification is in the best interests of the chills; and
(2) there is a substantial change in one (1) or more of the factors that the courts may consider under section 8 and, if applicable, section 8.5 of this chapter.

(b) In making its determination, the court shall consider the factors listed under section 8 of this chapter.

(c) The court shall not hear evidence on a matter occurring before the last custody proceeding between the parties unless the matter relates to a change in the factors relating to the best interests of the child as described by section 8 and, if applicable, section 8.5 of this chapter.
As added by P.L.1-1997, SEC.9. Amended by P.L.96-1999, SEC.9.

IC 31-17-2-21.5
Sec.21.5. The court may provide in:
 (1) a custody order; or
 (2) a modification to a custody order
for the security, bond, or other guarantee that is satisfactory to the
court to secure enforcement of the custody order.
As added by P.L.171-2001, SEC.11.

IC 31-17-2-21.7
Sec.21.7.(a) The court shall consider requiring security, a bond, or
another guarantee under section 21.5 of this chapter if the court
makes a finding under subdivision (1), (2), (4), or (7) by clear and
convincing evidence. If the court makes a finding under subdivision (1), (2), (4), or (7), the court shall also consider subdivisions
(3), (5), (6), (8), and (9) in determining the amount of security,
bond, or other guarantee. In making a determination under this
section, the court shall consider the following:
 (1) Whether a party has previously taken a child out of Indiana or
another state in violation of a custody or visitation order.
 (2) Whether a party has previously threatened to take a child out
of Indiana or another state in violation of a custody or visitation
order.
 (3) Whether a party has strong ties to Indiana.
 (4) Whether a party:
  (A) is a citizen of another country;
  (B) has strong emotional or cultural ties to the other country;
  and
  (C) has indicated or threatened to take a child out of Indiana to
  the other country.
 (5) Whether a party has friends or family living outside Indiana.
 (6) Whether a party does not have a financial reason to stay in
Indiana, such as whether the party is unemployed, able to work
anywhere, or is financially independent.
 (7) Whether a party has engaged in planning that would facilitate
removal from Indiana, such as quitting a job, selling the party's
primary residence, terminating a lease, closing an account, liqui-
dating other assets, hiding or destroying documents, applying for

a passport, applying for a birth certificate, or applying for school or medical records.

(8) Whether a party has a history of marital instability, a lack of parental cooperation, domestic violence, or child abuse.

(9) Whether a party has a criminal record.

After considering evidence, the court shall issue a written determination of security, bond, or other written guarantee supported by findings of fact and conclusions of law.

(b) If a motion for change of judge or change of venue, consider security, bond, or other guarantee under this chapter.

As added by P.L.171-2001, SEC.12.

IC 31-17-2-23

Sec.23.(a) If an individual who has been awarded custody of a child under this chapter intends to move a residence:

(1) other than a residence specified in the custody order; and

(2) that is outside Indiana or at least on hundred (100) miles from the individual's county of residence; the individual must file a notice of the intent to move with the clerk of the court that issued the custody order and send a copy of the notice to a parent who was not awarded custody and who has been granted visitation rights under IC 31-17-4 (or IC 31-1-11.5-24 before its repeal).

(b) Upon request of either party, the court shall set the matter for a hearing for the purposes of reviewing and modifying, if appropriate, the custody, visitation, and support orders. The court shall take into account the following in determining whether to modify the custody, visitation, and support orders:

(1) The distance involved in the proposed change of residence.

(2) the hardship and expense involved for noncustodial parents to exercise visitation rights.

(c) Except in cases of extreme hardship, the court may not award attorney's fees.

As added by P.L.1-1997, SEC.9. Amended by P.L.96-1999, SEC.10.

IC 31-17-2-24

Sec.24.(a) If either party to the custody order applies for a passport for the child, the party who applies for the child's passport shall do the following not less than ten (10) days before applying for the child's passport:

(1) File a notice of the passport application with the clerk of the court that issued the custody order.

(2) Send a copy of the notice to the other party.

(b) The parties may jointly agree in writing to waive the requirements of subsection (a).

As added by P.L.1-1997, SEC.9.

CRIMINAL LAW

▶DRIVING WHILE INTOXICATED

IN ST 9-30-5-1
IC 9-30-5-1 Class C misdemeanor; defense
Sec.1.(a) A person who operates a vehicle with an alcohol concentration equivalent to at least eight-hundredths (0.08) gram of alcohol but less than fifteen-hundredths (0.15) gram of alcohol per:

(1) one hundred (100) milliliters of the person's blood; or

(2) two hundred ten (210) liters of the person's breath;
commits a Class C misdemeanor.

(b) A person who operates a vehicle with an alcohol concentration equivalent to at least fifteen-hundredths (0.15) gram of alcohol per:

(1) one hundred (100) milliliters of the person's blood: or

(2) two hundred ten (210) liters of the person's breath;
commits a Class A misdemeanor.

(c) A person who operates a vehicle with a controlled substance listed in schedule I or II of IC 35-48-2 or its metabolite in the person's body commits a Class C misdemeanor.

(d) It is a defense to subsection (c) that the accused person consumed the controlled substance under a valid prescription or order of a practitioner (as defined in IC 35-48-1) who acted in the course of the practitioner's professional practice.

IN ST 9-30-5-2
IC 9-30-5-2 Class A misdemeanor

Sec.2.(a) Except as provided in subsection (b), a person who operates a vehicle while intoxicated commits a Class C misdemeanor.

(b) An offense described in subsection (a) is a Class A misdemeanor if the person operates a vehicle in a manner that endangers a person.

IN ST 9-30-5-3
IC 9-30-5-3 Class D felony; previous convictions
Sec.3. A person who violates section 1 or 2 of this chapter commits a Class D felony if:

(1) the person has a previous conviction of operating while intoxicated; and

(2) the previous conviction of operating while intoxicated occurred within the five (5) years immediately preceding the occurrence of the violation of section 1 or 2 of this chapter.

IN ST 9-30-5-4
IC 9-30-5-4 Classification of offense; serious bodily injury
Sec.4.(a) A person who causes serious bodily injury to another person when operating a motor vehicle:

(1) with an alcohol concentration equivalent to at least eight-hundredths (0.08) gram of alcohol per:

(A) one hundred (100) milliliters of the person's blood; or

(B) two hundred ten (210) liters of the person's breath;

(2) with a controlled substance listed in schedule I or II of IC 35-48-2 or its metabolite in the person's body; or

(3) while intoxicated

IN ST 9-30-5-5
IC 9-30-5-5 Classification of offense; death
Sec.5.(a) A person who causes the death of another person when operating a motor vehicle:

(1) with an alcohol concentration equivalent to at least eight-hundredths (0.08) gram of alcohol per:

(A) one hundred (100) milliliters of the person's blood; or

(B) two hundred ten (210) liters of the person's breath;

(2) with a controlled substance listed in schedule I or II of IC 35-

48-2 or its metabolite in the person's body; or
(3) while intoxicated

IN ST 9-30-5-6
IC 9-30-5-6 Class C infraction; violation of probationary license
Sec.6.(a) A person who operates a vehicle of any term of a probationary license issued under this chapter, IC 9-30-6, or IC 9-30-9 commits a Class C infraction.

(b) In addition to any other penalty imposed under this section, the court may suspend the person's driving privileges for a period of not more than one (1) year.

(C) The bureau shall send notice of a judgment entered under this section to the court that granted the defendant probationary driving privileges.

► *FELONIES*

IC 35-50-2-1
Sec.1.(a) As used in this chapter, "Class D felony conviction" means a conviction of a Class D felony in Indiana and a conviction, in any other jurisdiction at any time, with respect to which the convicted person might have been imprisoned for more than one (1) year. However, it does not include a conviction with respect to which the person has been pardoned, or a conviction of a Class A misdemeanor under section 7(b) of this chapter.

(b) As used in this chapter, "felony conviction" means a conviction, in any jurisdiction at any time, with respect to which the convicted person might have been imprisoned for more than one (1) year. However, it does not include a conviction with respect to which the person has been pardoned, or a conviction of a Class A misdemeanor under section 7(b) of this chapter.

(c) As used in this chapter, "minimum sentence" means:
  (1) for murder, forty-five (45) years;
  (2) for a Class A felony, twenty (20) years;
  (3) for a Class B felony, six (6) years;
  (4) for a Class C felony, two (2) years; and
  (5) for a Class D felony, one-half (1/2) year.

As added by Acts 1976, P.L.148, SEC.8. Amended by Acts 1977, P.L.340, SEC.114; P.L.334-1983, SEC.1; P.L.98-1988, SEC.8; P.L.243-2001, SEC.2 and P.L.291-2001, SEC.225.

IC 35-50-2-1.5
Sec.1.5. As used in this chapter, "mentally retarded individual" has the meaning set forth in IC 35-36-9-2.
As added by P.L.158-1994, SEC.4.

IC 35-50-2-2
Sec.2.(a) The court may suspend any part of a sentence for a felony, except as provided in this section or in section 2.1 of this chapter.

(b) With respect to the following crimes listed in this subsection, the court may suspend only that part of the sentence that is in excess of the minimum sentence:

(1) The crime committed was a Class A or Class B felony and the person has a prior unrelated felony conviction.

(2) The crime committed was a Class C felony and less than seven (7) years have elapsed between the date the person was discharged from probation, imprisonment, or parole, whichever is later, for a prior unrelated felony conviction and the date the person committed the Class C felony for which the person is being sentenced.

(3) The crime committed was a Class D felony and less than three (3) years have elapsed between the date the person was discharged from probation, imprisonment, or parole, whichever is later, for a prior unrelated conviction and the date the person committed the Class D felony for what the person is being sentenced. However, the court may suspend the minimum sentence for the crime only if the court orders home detention under IS 35-38-1-21 or IC 35-38-2.5-5 instead of the minimum sentence specified for the crime under this chapter.

(4) The felony committed was:
(A) murder (IC 35-42-1-1);
(B) battery (IC 35-42-2-1) with a deadly weapon or battery causing death;
(C) sexual battery (IC 35-42-4-8) with a deadly weapon;
(D) kidnapping (IC 35-42-3-2);

(E) confinement (IC 35-42-3-3) with a deadly weapon;

(F) rape (IC 35-42-4-1) as a Class A felony;

(G) criminal deviate conduct (IC 35-42-4-2) as a Class A felony;

(H) child molesting (IC 35-42-4-3) as a Class A or Class B felony;

(I) robbery (IC 35-42-5-1) resulting in serious bodily injury or with a deadly weapon;

(J) arson (IC 35-43-1-1) for hire or resulting in serious bodily injury;

(K) burglary (IC 35-43-2-1) resulting in serious bodily injury or with a deadly weapon;

(L) resisting law enforcement (IC 35-44-3-3) with a deadly weapon;

(M) escape (IC 35-44-3-5) with a deadly weapon;

(N) rioting (IC 35-45-1-2) with a deadly weapon;

(O) dealing in cocaine, a narcotic drug, or methamphetamine (IC 35-48-4-1) if the court finds the person possessed a firearm (as defined in IC 35-47-1-5) at the time of the offense, or the person delivered or intended to deliver to a person under eighteen (18) years of age at least three (3) years junior to the person and was on a school bus or within one thousand (1,000) feet of :

  (i) school property;

  (ii) a public park;

  (iii) a family housing complex; or

  (iv) a youth program center;

(P) dealing in a schedule I, II, or III controlled substance (IC 35-48-4-2) if the court finds the person possessed a firearm (as defined in IC 35-47-1-5) at the time of the offense, or the person delivered or intended to deliver to a person under eighteen (18) years of age at least three (3) years junior to the person and was on a school bus or within one thousand (1,000) feet of:

  (i) school property;

  (ii) a public park;

  (iii) a family housing complex; or

  (iv) a youth program center;

(Q) an offense under IC 9-30-5 (operating a vehicle while intoxicated) and the person who committed the offense has accumulated at least two (2) prior unrelated convictions under 9-30-5; or

(R) aggravated battery (IC 35-42-2-1.5).

(c) Except as provided in subsection (e), whenever the court suspends a sentence for a felony, it shall place the person on probation under IC 35-38-2 for a fixed period to end not later than the date that the maximum sentence that may be imposed or the felony will expire.

(d) The minimum sentence for a person convicted of voluntary manslaughter may not be suspended unless the court finds at the sentencing hearing that the crime was not committed by means of a deadly weapon.

(e) Whenever the court suspends that part of a sex and violent offender's (as defined in IC 5-2-12-4) sentence that is suspendible under subsection (b), the court shall place the offender on probation under IC 35-38-2 for not more than ten (10) years.

(f) An additional term of imprisonment imposed under IC 35-50-2-11 may not be suspended.

(g) A term of imprisonment imposed under IC 35-47-10-6 or IC 35-47-10-7 may not be suspended if the commission of the offense was knowing or intentional.

(h) A term of imprisonment imposed for an offense under IC 35-48-4-6(b)(1)(B) may not be suspended.

As added by Acts 1976, P.L.148. SEC.8. Amended by Acts 1977, P.L.340, SEC.115; Acts 1979, P.L.305, SEC.1; Acts 1982, P.L.204, SEC.39; P.L.334-1983, SEC.2; P.L.284-1985, SEC.3; P.L.,211-1986, SEC.1; P.l.98-1988, SEC.9; P.L.351-1989(ss), SEC.4; P.L.214-1991, SEC.2; P.L.240-1991(ss2), SEC.98; P.L.11-1994, SEC.17; P.L.203-1996, SEC.8; P.L.96-1996, SEC.7; P.L.220-1997, SEC.1; P.L.188-1999, SEC.8; P.L.17-2001, SEC.30; P.L.222-2001, SEC.6; P.L.238-2001, SEC.21.

IC 35-50-2-2.1
Sec.2.1.(a) Except as provided in subsection (b) or section 2 of this chapter, the court may not suspend a sentence for a felony for a person with a juvenile record when:
(1) the juvenile records includes findings that the juvenile acts, if committed by an adult, would constitute:
(A) one (1) Class A or Class B felony;
(B) two (2) Class C or Class D felonies;

(C) one (1) Class C and one (1) Call D felony; and

(2) less than three (3) years have elapsed between commission of the juvenile acts that would be felonies if committed by an adult and the commission of the felony for which the person is being sentenced.

(b) Notwithstanding subsection (a), the court may suspend any part of the sentence for a felony, except as provided in section 2 of this chapter, if it finds that:

(1) the crime was the result of circumstances unlikely to recur;

(2) the victim of the crime induced or facilitated the offense;

(3) there are substantial grounds tending to excuse or justify the crime, though failing to establish a defense; or

(4) the acts in the juvenile records would not be a Class A or Class B felonies if committed by an adult, and the convicted person is to undergo home detention under IC 35-38-1-21 instead of the minimum sentence specified for the crime under this chapter.

As added by P.L.284-1985, SEC.4. Amended by P.L.331-1987, SEC.1; P.L.98-1988, SEC.10.

IC 35-50-2-3

Sec.3.(a) A person who commits murder shall be imprisoned for a fixed term of fifty-five (55) years, with not more than ten (10) years added for aggravating circumstances or not more than ten (10) years subtracted for mitigating circumstances; in addition, the person may be fined not more than ten thousand dollars ($10,000).

(b) Notwithstanding subsection (a), a person who was at least sixteen (16) years of age at the time the murder was committed may be sentenced to:

(1) death; or

(2) life imprisonment without parole;

under section 9 of this chapter unless a court determines under IC 35-36-9 that the person is a mentally retarded individual.

As added by Acts 1976, P.L.148, SEC.8. Amended by Acts 1977, P.L.340, SEC.116; P.L.332-1987, SEC.1; P.L.250-1993, SEC.1; P.L.164-1994, SEC.2; P.L.158-1994, SEC.5; P.L.2-1995, SEC,128; P.L.148-1995, SEC.4.

IC 35-50-2-4

Sec.4. A person who commits a Class A felony shall be imprisoned for a fixed term of thirty (30) years, with not more than twenty (20) years added for aggravating circumstances or not more than ten (10) years subtracted for mitigating circumstances; in addition, he may be fined not more than ten thousand dollars ($10,000).
As added by Acts 1976, P.L.148, SEC.8. Amended by Acts 1977, P.L.340, SEC.118.

IC 35-50-2-6
Sec.6.(a) A person who commits a Class C felony shall be imprisoned for a fixed term of four (4) years, with not more than four (4) years added for aggravating circumstances or not more than two (2) years subtracted for mitigating circumstances. In addition, he may be fined not more than ten thousand dollars ($10,000).

(b) Notwithstanding subsection (a), if a person has committed non-support of a child as a Class C felony under IC 35-46-1-5, upon motion of the prosecuting attorney, the court may enter judgment of conviction of a Class D felony under IC 35-46-1-5 and sentence the person accordingly. The court shall enter in the record detailed reasons for the court's action when the court enters a judgment of conviction of a Class D felony under this subsection.
As added by Acts 1976, P.P.148, SEC.8. Amended by Acts 1977, P.L.340, SEC.119; P.L.167-1990, SEC.1; P.L.213-1996, SEC.5.

IC 35-50-2-7
Sec.7.(a) A person who commits a Class D felony shall be imprisoned for a fixed term of one and one-half (1 +) years, with not more than one and one-half (1 +) years added for aggravating circumstances or not more than one (1) year subtracted for mitigating circumstances. In addition, he may be fined not more than ten thousand dollars ($10,000).

(b) Notwithstanding subsection (a), if a person has committed a Class D felony, the court may enter judgment of conviction of a Class A misdemeanor and sentence accordingly. However, the court shall enter a judgment of conviction of a Class D felony if:
  (1) the court finds that:
    (A) the person has committed a prior, unrelated felony for which

judgment was entered as a conviction of a Class A misdemeanor; and

(B) the prior felony was committed less than three (3) years before the second felony was committed;

(2) the offense is domestic battery as a Class D felony under IC 35-42-2-1.3;

(3) the offense is auto theft (IC 35-43-2.5); or

(4) the offense is receiving stolen auto parts (IC 35-43-4-2.5).

The court shall enter in the record, in detail, the reason for its action whenever it exercises the power to enter judgment of conviction of a Class A misdemeanor granted in this subsection.

As added by Acts 1976, P.L.148, SEC.8. Amended by Acts 1977, P.L.340, SEC.120; Acts 1982, P.L.204, SEC.40; P.L.334-1983, SEC.3; P.L.136-1987, SEC.7; P.L.167-1990, SEC.2; P.L.188-1999, SEC.9.

IC 35-50-2-7.1 Repealed
Repealed by P.L.164-1993, SEC.14.

IC 35-50-2-8
Sec.8.(a) Except as otherwise provided in this section, the state may seek to have a person sentenced as a habitual offender for any felony by alleging, on a page separate from the rest of the charging instrument, that the person has accumulated two (2) prior unrelated felony convictions.

(b) The state may not seek to have a person sentenced as a habitual offender for a felony offense under this section if:

(1) the offense is a misdemeanor that is enhanced to a felony in the same proceeding as the habitual offender proceeding solely because the person had a prior unrelated conviction;

(2) the offense is an offense under IC 9-30-10-16 or IC 9-30-10-17; or

(3) all of the following apply:

(A) The offense is an offense under IC 16-42-19 or IC 35-48-4.

(B) The offense is not listed in section 2(b)(4) of this chapter.

(C) The total number of unrelated convictions that the person has for:

(i) dealing in or selling a legend drug under IC 16-42-19-27;

(ii) dealing in cocaine or a narcotic drug (IC 35-48-4-1);

(iii) dealing in a schedule I, II, III controlled substance (IC 35-48-4-2);

(iv) dealing in a schedule IV controlled substance (IC 35-48-4-3); and

(v) dealing in a schedule V controlled substance (IC 35-48-4-4);

does not exceed one (1).

(c) A person has accumulated two (2) prior unrelated felony convictions for purposes of this section only if:

(1) the second prior unrelated felony conviction was committed after sentencing for the first prior unrelated felony conviction; and

(2) the offense for which the state seeks to have the person sentenced as a habitual offender was committed after sentencing for the second prior unrelated felony conviction.

(d) A conviction does not count for purposes of this section as a prior unrelated felony conviction if:

(1) the conviction has been set aside;

(2) the conviction is one for which the person has been pardoned; or

(3) all of the following apply:

(A) The offense is an offense under IC 16-42-19 or IC 35-48-4.

(B) The offense is not listed in section 2(b)(4) of this chapter.

(C) The total number of unrelated convictions that the person has for:

(i) dealing in or selling a legend drug under IC 16-42-19-27;

(ii) dealing in cocaine or a narcotic drug (IC 35-48-4-1);

(iii) dealing in a schedule I, II, III controlled substance (IC 35-48-4-2);

(iv) dealing in a schedule V controlled substance (IC 35-48-4-4);

does not exceed one (1).

(e) The requirements in subsections (b) do not apply to a prior unrelated felony conviction that is used to support a sentence as a habitual offender. A prior unrelated felony conviction may be used under this section to support a sentence as a habitual offender even if the sentence for the prior unrelated offense was enhanced for any reason, including an enhancement because the person has been convicted of another offense. However, a prior unrelated felony conviction under IC 9-30-10-16, IC 9-30-10-17, IC 9-12-3-1 (repealed), or IC 9-12-3-2 (repealed) may not be used to support a sentence as a habitual offender.

(f) If the person was convicted of the felony in a jury trial, the jury shall reconvene for the sentencing hearing. If the trial was to the court or the judgment was entered on a guilty plea, the court alone shall conduct the sentencing hearing under IC 35-38-1-3.

(g) A person is a habitual offender if the jury (if the hearing is by jury) or the court (if the hearing is to the court alone) finds that the state has proved beyond a reasonable doubt that the person had accumulated two (2) prior unrelated felony convictions.

(h) The court shall sentence a person found to be a habitual offender to an additional fixed term that is not less than the presumptive sentence for the underlying offense nor more than three (3) times the presumptive sentence for the underlying offense. However, the additional sentence may not exceed thirty (3) years.

As added by Acts 1976, P.L.148, SEC.8. Amended by Acts 1977, P.L.340, SEC.121; Acts 1980, P.L.210, SEC.1; P.L.335-1983, SEC.1; P.L.328-1985, SEC.2; P.L.1-1990, SEC.353; P.L.164-1993, SEC.13; P.L.140-1994, SEC.14; P.L.305-1995, SEC.1; P.L.166-2001, SEC.3; P.L.291-2001, SEC.226.

IC 35-50-2-8.5
Sec.8.5(a) The state may seek to have a person sentenced to life imprisonment without parole for any felony described in section 2(b)(4) of this chapter by alleging, on a page separate from the rest of the charging instrument, that the person has accumulated two (2) prior unrelated felony convictions described in section 2(b)(4) of this chapter.

(b) If the person was convicted of the felony in a jury trial, the jury shall reconvene to hear evidence on the life imprisonment without parole allegation. If the person was convicted of the felony by trial to the court without a jury or if the judgment was entered to guilty plea, the court alone shall hear evidence on the life imprisonment without parole allegation.

(c) A person is subject to life imprisonment without parole if the jury (in a case tried by a jury) or the court (in a case tried by the court or on a judgment entered on a guilty plea) finds that the state has proved beyond a reasonable doubt that the person has accumulated two (2) prior unrelated convictions for offenses described in section 2(b)(4) of this chapter.

(d) The court may sentence a person found to be subject to life imprisonment without parole under this section to life imprisonment without parole.

As added by P.L.158-1994, SEC.6.

IC 35-50-2-9
Sec.9.(a) The state may seek either a death sentence or a sentence of life imprisonment without parole for murder by alleging, on a page separate from the rest of the charging instrument, the existence of at least one (1) of the aggravating circumstances listed in subsection (b). In the sentencing hearing after a person is convicted of murder, the state must prove beyond a reasonable doubt the existence of at least one (1) of the aggravating circumstances alleged. However, the state may not proceed against a defendant under this section if a court determines at a pretrial hearing under IC 35-36-9 that the defendant is a mentally retarded individual.

(b) The aggravating circumstances are as follows:

(1) The defendant committed the murder by intentionally killing the victim while committing or attempting to commit any of the following:

(A) Arson (IC 35-43-1-1).

(B) Burglary (IC 35-43-2-1).

(C) Child molesting (IC 35-42-4-3).

(D) Criminal deviate conduct (IC 35-42-4-2).

(E) Kidnapping (IC 35-42-3-2).

(F) Rape (IC 35-42-4-1).

(G) Robbery (IC 35-42-5-1).

(H) Carjacking (IC 35-42-5-2).

(I) Criminal gang activity (IC 35-45-9-3).

(J) Dealing in cocaine or a narcotic drug (IC 35-48-4-1).

(2) The defendant committed the murder by the unlawful detona-

188

tion of an explosive with intent to injure person or damage property.

(3) The defendant committed the murder by lying in wait.

(4) The defendant who committed the murder was hire to kill.

(5) The defendant committed the murder by hiring another person to kill.

(6) The victim of the murder was a corrections employee, probation officer, parole officer, community corrections worker, home detention officer, fireman, judge, or law enforcement officer, and either:

(A) the victim was acting in the course of duty; or

(B) the murder was motivated by an act the victim performed while acting in the course of duty.

(7) The defendant has been convicted of another murder.

(8) The defendant has committed another murder, at any time, regardless of whether the defendant has been convicted of that other murder.

(9) The defendant was:

(A) under the custody of the department of corrections;

(B) under the custody of a county sheriff;

(C) on probation after receiving a sentence for the commission of a felony; or

(D) on parole;

at the time the murder was committed.

(10) The defendant dismembered the victim.

(11) The defendant burned, mutilated, or tortured the victim while the victim was alive.

(12) The victim of the murder was less than twelve (12) years of age.

(13) They victim was a victim of any of the following offenses for which the defendant was convicted:

(A) Battery as a Class D felony or as a Class C felony under IC 35-42-2-1.

(B) Kidnapping (IC 35-42-3-2).

(C) Criminal confinement (IC 35-42-3-3).

(D) a sex crime under IC 35-42-4.

(14) The victim of the murder was listed by the state or known by

the defendant to be a witness against the defendant and the defendant committed the murder with the intent to prevent the person from testifying.

(15) The defendant committed the murder by intentionally discharging a firearm (as defined in IC 35-47-1-5):

  (A) into an inhabited dwelling; or

  (B) from a vehicle.

(16) The victim of the murder was pregnant and the murder resulted in the intentional killing of a fetus that has attained viability (as defined in IC 16-18-2-365).

(c) The mitigating circumstances that may be considered under this section are as follows:

(1) The defendant has no significant history of prior criminal conduct.

(2) The defendant was under the influence of extreme mental or emotional disturbance when the murder was committed.

(3) The victim was a participant in or consented to the defendant's conduct.

(4) The defendant was an accomplice in a murder committed by another person, and the defendant's participation was relatively minor.

(5) The defendant acted under the substantial domination of another person.

(6) The defendant's capacity to appreciate the criminality of the defendant's conduct or to conform that conduct to the requirements of law was substantially impaired as a result of mental disease or defect or of intoxication.

(7) The defendant was less than eighteen (18) years of age at the time the murder was committed.

(8) Any other circumstances appropriate for consideration.

(d) If the defendant was convicted of murder in a jury trial, the jury shall reconvene for the sentencing hearing. If the trial was to the court, or the judgment was entered on a guilty plea, the court alone shall conduct the sentencing hearing. The jury or the court may consider all the evidence introduced at the trial stage of the proceedings, together with new evidence presented at the sentencing hearing. The court shall instruct the jury concerning the statutory penalties for murder and any other offenses for which the defendant was convicted, the potential for consecutive or concurrent sentencing, and the availability of good time credit and clemency. The defendant may present any additional evidence relevant to:

(1) the aggravating circumstances alleged; or

(2) any of the mitigating circumstances listed in subsection (c).

(e) Except as provided by IC 35-36-9, if the hearing is by jury, the jury shall recommend to the court whether the death penalty or life imprisonment without parole, or neither, should be imposed. The jury may recommend:

(1) the death penalty; or

(2) life imprisonment without parole;

only if it makes the findings described in subsection (k). The court shall make the final determination of the sentence, after considering the jury's recommendation, and the sentence shall be based on the same standards that the jury was required to consider. The court is not bound by the jury's recommendation. In making the final determination of the sentence after receiving the jury's recommendation, the court may receive evidence of the crime's impact on members of the victim's family.

(f) If a jury is unable to agree on a sentence recommendation after reasonable deliberations, the court shall discharge the jury and proceed as if the hearing had been to the court alone.

(g) If the hearing is to the court alone, except as provided by IC 35-36-9, the court shall:

(1) sentence the defendant to death; or

(2) impose a term of life imprisonment without parole;

only if it meets the findings described in subsection (k).

(h) If a court sentences a defendant to death, the court shall order the defendant's execution to be carried out not later than one (1) year and one (1) day after the date the defendant was convicted. The supreme court has exclusive jurisdiction to stay the execution of a death sentence. If the supreme court stays the execution of a death sentence, the supreme court shall order a new date for the defendant's execution.

(i) If a person sentenced to death by a court files a petition for post-conviction relief, the court, not later than ninety (90) days after the date the petition is filed, shall set a date to hold a hearing to consider the petition. If a court does not, within the ninety (90) day period, set the date to hold the hearing to consider the petition, the court's failure to set the hearing date is not a basis for additional post-conviction relief. The attorney general shall answer the petition for post-conviction relief on behalf of the state. At the request of the attorney general, a prosecuting attorney shall assist the attorney general. The court shall enter written findings of fact and conclusions of law concerning the petition not later than ninety (90) days after the date the hearing concludes. However, if the court determines that the petition is without merit, the court may dismiss the petition within ninety (90) days without conducting a hearing under this subsection.

(j) A death sentence is subject to automatic review by the supreme court. The review, which shall be heard under rules adopted by the supreme court, shall be given priority over all other cases. The supreme court's review must take into consideration all claims that the :

(1) conviction or sentence was in violation of the:

(A) Constitution of the State of Indiana; or

(B) Constitution of the United States;

(2) sentencing court was without jurisdiction to impose a sentence; and

(3) sentence:

(A) exceeds the maximum sentence authorized by law; or

(B) is otherwise erroneous.

If the supreme court cannot complete its review by the date set by the sentencing court for the defendant's execution under subsection (h), the supreme court shall stay the execution of the death sentence and set a new date to carry out the defendant's execution.

(k) Before a sentence may be imposed under this section, the jury, in a proceeding under subsection (e), or the court, in a proceeding under subsection (g), must find that:

(1) the state has proved beyond a reasonable doubt that at least

one (1) of the aggravating circumstances listed in subsection (b) exists; and

(2) any mitigating circumstances that exist are outweighed by the aggravating circumstance or circumstances.

As added by Acts 1977, P.L.340, SEC.122. Amended by P.L.336-1983, SEC.1; P.L.212-1986, SEC.1; P.L.332-1987, SEC.2; P.L.320-1987, SEC.2; P.L.296-1989, SEC.1; P.L.138-1989, SEC.6; P.L.1-1990, SEC.354; P.L.230-1993, SEC.5; P.L.250-1993, SEC.2; P.L.158-1994, SEC.7; P.L.306-1995, SEC.1; P.L.228, 1006, SEC.1; P.L.216-1996, SEC.25; P.L.261-1997, SEC.7.

IC 35-50-2-10

Sec.10.(a) As used in this section:

(1) "Drug" means a drug or a controlled substance (as defined in IC 35-48-1).

(2) "Substance offense" means a Class A misdemeanor or a felony in which the possession, use, abuse, delivery, transportation, or manufacture of alcohol or drugs is a material element of the crime. The term includes an offense under IC 9-30-5 and an offense under IC 9-11-2 (before it repeal July 1, 1991).

(b) The state may seek to have a person sentenced as a habitual substance offender for any substance offense by alleging, on a page separate from the rest of the charging instrument, that the person has accumulated two (2) prior unrelated substance offense convictions.

(c) After a person has been convicted and sentenced for a substance offense committed after sentencing for a prior unrelated substance offense conviction, the person has accumulated two (2) prior unrelated substance offense convictions. However, a conviction does not count for purposes of this subsection if:

(1) it has been set aside; or

(2) it is a conviction for whish the person has been pardoned.

(d) If the person was convicted of the substance offense in a jury trial, the jury shall reconvene for the sentencing hearing. If the trial was to the court, or the judgment was entered on a guilty plea, the court alone shall conduct the sentencing hearing, under IC 35-38-1-3.

(e) A person is a habitual substance offender if the jury (if the hearing is by jury) or the court (if the hearing is to the court alone) finds that the state has proved beyond a reasonable doubt that the person had accumulated two (2) prior unrelated substance offense convictions.

(f) The court shall sentence a person found to be a habitual substance offender to an additional fixed term of at least three (3) years but not more than eight (8) years imprisonment, to be added to the term of imprisonment imposed under IC 35-50-2 or IC 35-50-3. If the court finds that:

(1) three (3) years or more have elapsed since the date the person was discharged from probation, imprisonment, or parole, (whichever is later) for the last prior unrelated substance offense conviction and the date the person committed the substance offense for which the person is being sentenced as a habitual substance offender; or

(2) all of the substance offenses for which the person has been convicted are substance offenses under IC 16-42-19 or IC 35-48-4, the person has not been convicted of a substance offense listed in section 2(b)(4) of this chapter, and the total number of convictions that the person has for:

(A) dealing in or selling a legend drug under IC 16-42-19-27;

(B) dealing in cocaine or a narcotic drug (IC 35-48-4-1);

(C) dealing in a schedule I, II, or III controlled substance (IC 35-48-4-2);

(D) dealing in a schedule IV controlled substance (IC 35-48-4-3); and

(E) dealing in a schedule V controlled substance (IC 35-48-4-4);
does not exceed one (1);
then the court may reduce the additional fixed term. However, the court may not reduce the additional fixed term to less than one (1) year.

(g) If a reduction of the additional year fixed term is authorized under subsection (f), the court may also consider the aggravating or mitigating circumstances in IC 35-38-1-7.1 to:

(1) decide the issued of granting a reduction; or

(2) determine the number of years, if any, to be subtracted, under subsection (f).

As added by P.L.335-1983, SEC.2. Amended by P.L.327-1985, SEC.5; P.L.98-1988, SEC.11; P.L.1-1990, SEC.355; P.L.96-1996, SEC.8; P.L.97-1996, SEC.5; P.L.2-1997, SEC.77; P.L.291-2001, SEC.227.

IC 35-50-2-11
Sec.11.(a) As used in this section, "firearm" has the meaning set forth in IC 35-47-1-5.

(b) As used in this section, "offense" means:
  (1) a felony under IC 35-42 that resulted in death or serious bodily injury;
  (2) kidnapping; or
  (3) criminal confinement as a Class B felony.

(c) The state may seek, on a page separate from the rest of a charging instrument, to have a person who allegedly committed an offense sentenced to an additional fixed term of imprisonment if the state can show beyond a reasonable doubt that the person knowingly or intentionally used a firearm in the commission of the offense.

(d) If after a sentencing hearing a court finds that a person who committed an offense used a firearm in the commission of the offense, the court may sentence the person to an additional fixed term of imprisonment of five (5) years.

As added by P.L.140-1994, SEC.15. Amended by P.L.203-1996, SEC.9.

IC 35-50-2-12
Sec.12. The Indiana criminal justice institute shall review characteristics of offenders committed to the department of correction over such period of time it deems appropriate and of the offenses committed by those offenders in order to ascertain norms used by the trial courts in sentencing. The Indiana criminal justice institute shall from time to time publish its findings in the Indiana Register and provide its findings to the legislative services agency and the judicial conference of Indiana.

As added by P.L.164-1994, SEC.4.

IC 35-50-2-13

Sec.13.(a) The state may seek, on a page separate from the rest of a charging instrument, to have a person who allegedly committed an offense of dealing in a controlled substance under IC 35-48-4-1 through IC 35-48-4-4 sentenced to an additional fixed term of imprisonment if the state can show beyond a reasonable doubt that the person knowingly or intentionally:

(1) used a firearm; or

(2) possessed a:

(A) handgun in violation of IC 35-47-2-1;

(B) sawed-off shotgun in violation of IC 35-47-5-4.1; or

(C) machine gun in violation of IC 35-47-5-8;

while committing the offense.

(b) If after a sentencing hearing a court finds that a person committed an offense as described in subsection (a), the court may sentence the person to an additional fixed term of imprisonment of not more than five (5) years, except as follows:

(1) If the firearm is a sawed-off shotgun, the court may sentence the person to an additional fixed term of imprisonment of not more than ten (10) years.

(2) If the firearm is a machine gun or is equipped with a firearm silencer or firearm muffler, the court may sentence the person to an additional fixed term of imprisonment of not more than twenty (20) years. The additional sentence under this subdivision is in addition to any additional sentence imposed under section 11 of this chapter for use of a firearm in the commission of an offense. *As added by P.L.148-1995, SEC.6.*

IC 35-50-2-14

Sec.14.(a) The state may seek to have a person sentenced as a repeat sexual offender for a sex offense under IC 35-42-4-1 through IC 35-42-4-9 or IC 35-46-1-3 by alleging, on a page separate from the rest of the charging instrument, that the person has accumulated one (1) prior unrelated felony conviction for a sex offense under IC 35-42-4-1 through IC 35-42-4-9 or IC 35-46-1-3.

(b) After a person has been convicted and sentenced for a felony committed after sentencing for a prior unrelated felony conviction

under IC 35-42-4-1 through IC 35-42-4-9 or IC 35-46-1-3, the person has accumulated one (1) prior unrelated felony conviction. However, a conviction does not count for purposes of this subsection, if:
  (1) it has been set aside; or
  (2) it is one for which the person has been pardoned.
(c) The court alone shall conduct the sentencing hearing under IC 35-38-1-3.

(d) A person is a repeat sexual offender if the court finds that the state has proved beyond a reasonable doubt that the person had accumulated one (1) prior unrelated felony conviction under IC 35-42-4-1 through IC 35-42-4-9 or IC 35-46-1-3.

(e) The court may sentence a person found to be a repeat sexual offender to an additional fixed term that is the presumptive sentence for the underlying offense. However, the additional sentence may not exceed ten (10) years.
As added by P.L.214-1999, SEC.4.

REAL ESTATE

▶*BUYING AND SELLING REAL ESTATE*

IC 24-4.6-2-2
Sec.2. As used in this chapter, "buyer" means a transferee in a transaction described in section 1 of this chapter.
As added by P.L.209-1993, SEC.1.

IC 24-4.6-2-3
Sec.3. As used in this chapter, "closing" means a transfer of an interest described in section 1 of this chapter by a deed, installment sales contract, or lease.
As added by P.L.209-1993, SEC.1.

IC 24-4.6-2-4
Sec.4. As used in connection with disclosure forms required by this chapter, "defect" means a condition that would have a significant adverse effect on the value of the property, that would significantly impair the health or safety of future occupants of the property, or

that if not repaired, removed or replaced would significantly shorten or adversely affect the expected normal life of the premises.
As added by P.L.209-1993, SEC.1.

IC 24-4.6-2-5
Sec.5. As used in this chapter, "disclosure form" refers to a disclosure form prepared under section 7 of this chapter or a disclosure from that meets the requirements of section 8 of the chapter.
As added by P.L.209-1993, SEC.1.

IC 24-4.6-2-6
Sec.6. As used in this chapter, "owner" means the owner of the residential real estate that is for sale, exchange, lease with an option to buy, or sale under an installment contract.
As added by P.L.209-1993, SEC.1.

IC 24-4.6-2-7
Sec.7. The Indiana real estate commission established by IC 25-34.2-2-1 shall adopt a specific disclosure form that contains that following:
(1) Disclosure by the owner of the known condition of the following areas:
   (A) The foundation.
   (B) The mechanical systems.
   (C) The roof.
   (D) The structure.
   (E) The water and sewer systems.
   (F) Other areas that the Indiana real estate commission determines are appropriate.
(2) A notice to the prospective buyer that contains substantially the following language:
"The prospective buyer and the owner may wish to obtain professional advice or inspections of the property and provide for appropriate provisions in a contract between them concerning any advice, inspections, defects, or warranties obtained on the property.".
(3) A notice to the prospective buyer that contains substantially the following language:

"The representatives in this form are the representative of the owner and are not the representatives of the agent, if any. This information is for disclosure only and is not intended to be a part of any contract between the buyer and owner."

(4) A disclosure by the owner that an airport is located within a geographical distance from the property as determined by the Indiana real estate commission. The commission may consider the differences between an airport serving commercial airlines and an airport that does not serve commercial airlines in determining the distance to be disclosed.

As added by P.L.209-1993, SEC.1. Amended by P.L.232-1995, SEC.1.

IC 24-4.6-2-8
Sec.8. An owner may prepare or use a disclosure form that contains the information in the disclosure form under section 7 of this chapter and any other information the owner determines is appropriate.
As added by P.L.209-1993, SEC.1.

IC 24-4.6-2-9
Sec.9. A disclosure form is not a warranty by the owner or the owner's agent, if any, and the disclosure form may not be used as a substitute for any inspections or warranties that the prospective buyer or owner may later obtain.
As added by P.L.209-1993, SEC.1.

IC 24-4.6-2-10
Sec.10.(a) An owner must complete and sign a disclosure form and submit the form to a prospective buyer before an offer is accepted for the sale of the residential real estate.

(b) An appraiser retained to appraise the residential real estate for which the disclosure form has been prepared shall be given a copy of the form upon request. This subsection only applies to appraisals made for the buyer or an entity from which the buyer is seeking financing.

(c) An accepted offer is not enforceable against the buyer before closing until the owner and the prospective buyer have signed the disclosure form. After closing the failure of the owner to deliver a disclosure statement form to the buyer does not by itself invalidate a real estate transaction.

As added by P.L.209-1993, SEC.1.

IC 24-4.6-2-11

Sec.11. The owner is not liable for an error, inaccuracy, or omission of any information required to be delivered to the prospective buyer under this chapter if:

(1) the error, inaccuracy, or omission was not within the actual knowledge of the owner or was based on information provided by a public agency or by another person with a professional license or special knowledge who provided a written or oral report or opinion that the owner reasonably believed to be correct; and

(2) the owner was not negligent in obtaining information from a third party and transmitting the information.

As added by P.L.209-1993, SEC.1.

IC 24-4.6-2-12

Sec.12.(a) An owner does not violate this chapter if the owner subsequently discovers that the disclosure form is inaccurate as a result of any act, circumstance, information received, or agreement subsequent to the delivery of the disclosure form. However, at or before settlement, the owner is required to disclose any material change in the physical condition of the property or certify to the purchaser at settlement that the condition of the property is substantially the same as it was when the disclosure form was provided.

(b) If at the time disclosures are required to be made under subsection (a) an item of information required to be disclosed is unknown or not available to the owner, the owner may state that the information is unknown or may use an approximation of the information if the approximation is clearly identified, is reasonable, is based on the actual knowledge of the owner, and is not used to circumvent the disclosure requirements of this chapter.

As added by P.L.209-1993, SEC.2.

IC 24-4.6-2-13

Sec.13.(a) Notwithstanding section 12 of this chapter, if a prospective buyer receives a disclosure form or an amended disclosure form after an offer has been accepted that discloses a defect, the prospective buyer may after receipt of the disclosure form and within two (2) business days nullify the contract by delivering a written rescission to the owner or the owner's agent, if nay.

(b) A prospective buyer is not liable for nullifying a contract under this section and is entitled to a return of any deposits made in the transaction.
As added by P.L.209-1993, SEC.1.

▶ *TENANT AND LANDLORD RELATIONS*

IC 32-7-8-2
Sec.2.(a) For purposes of this section, "tenant" includes a former tenant.

(b) A waiver of this chapter by a landlord or tenant, by contract or otherwise, is void.
As added by P.L.180-1999, SEC.1.

IC 32-7-8-3
Sec.3. The definitions in IC 32-7-5 apply throughout this chapter.
As added by P.L.180-1999, SEC.1.

IC 32-7-8-4
Sec.4.(a) As used in this chapter, "dwelling unit" means a structure or part of a structure that is used as a home, residence, or sleeping unit.

(b) The term includes an apartment unit, a boarding house unit, a rooming house unit, a manufactured home (as defined in IC 22-12-1-16) or mobile structure (as defined in IC 22-12-1-17) used as a dwelling unit and the manufactured home's or mobile structure's space, and a single or two (2) family dwelling.
As added by P.L.180-1999, SEC.1.

IC 32-7-8-5
Sec.5. Unless otherwise provided by a written rental agreement between a landlord and tenant, a landlord shall give the tenant at least

thirty (30) days written notice before modifying the rental agreement.

As added by P.L.180-1999, SEC.1.

IC 32-7-8-6

Sec.6. Except as provided in IC 16-41-27-29, IC 32-7-5, or IC 32-7-6, a landlord may not:

(1) take possession of;

(2) remove from a tenant's dwelling unit;

(3) deny a tenant access to; or

(4) dispose of;

a tenant's personal property in order to enforce an obligation of the tenant to the landlord under a rental agreement. The landlord and tenant may agree in a writing separate from the rental agreement that the landlord may hold property voluntarily tendered by the tenant as security in exchange for forbearance from an action to evict.

As added by P.L.180-1999, SEC.1

IC 32-7-8-7

Sec.7.(a) This section does not apply if the dwelling unit has been abandoned.

(b) For purposes of this section, a dwelling unit is considered abandoned if:

(1) the tenants have failed to pay, or have failed to offer to pay, rent due under the rental agreement; and

(2) the circumstances are such that a reasonable person would conclude that the tenants have surrendered possession of the dwelling unit.

An oral or written rental agreement may not define abandonment differently than is provided by this subsection.

(c) Except as authorized by judicial order, a landlord may not deny or interfere with a tenant's access to or possession of the tenant's dwelling unit by commission of any act, including any of the following:

(1) Changing the locks or adding a device to exclude the tenant from the dwelling unit.

(2) Removing the doors, windows, fixtures, or appliances from the dwelling unit.

(3) Interrupting, reducing, shutting off, or causing termination of electricity, gas, water, or other essential services to the tenant unless the interruption, shutting off, or termination results from an emergency, good faith repairs, or necessary construction. This subdivision does not require a landlord to pay for services described in this subdivision if the landlord has not agreed, by an oral or written rental agreement, to do so.

(d) A tenant may not interrupt, reduce, shut off, or cause termination of electricity, gas, water, or other essential services to the dwelling unit if the interruption, reduction, shutting off, or termination of the services will result in serious damage to the rental unit.

As added by P.L.180-1999, SEC.1.

APPOINTMENT OF HEALTH CARE REPRESENTATIVE

I, _____ hereby appoint:

Principle Representative's Name _____

Address _____

Telephone _____

as my health care representative or representative to make health and personal care decisions for me as authorized in this document.

ALTERNATIVE REPRESENTATIVE

I revoke my Representative's authority; or my Representative becomes unwilling or unavailable to act; or if my Representative is my spouse and I become legally separated or divorced, I name the following (each to act along and successively, in the order named) as alternates to my Representative:

A. First Alternate Representative

Name _____

Address _____

Telephone _____

B. Second Alternate Representative

Name _____

Address _____

Telephone _____

EFFECTIVE DATE AND DURABILITY

By this document I intend to create a health care advance directive. It is effective upon, and only during, any period in which I cannot make or communicate a choice regarding a particular health care decision. My Representative, attending physician and any other necessary experts should determine that I am unable to make choices about health care.

REPRESENTATIVE'S POWERS

I give my Representative full authority to make health care decisions for me. My Representative shall follow my wishes as known to my Representative either through this document or through other means. When my Representative interprets my wishes, I intend my Representative's authority to be as broad as possible, except for any limitations I state in this form. In making any decisions, my Representative shall try to discuss the proposed decision with me to determine my desires if I am able to communicate in any way. If my Representative cannot determine the choice I would want, then my Representative shall make a choice for me based upon what my Representative believes to be in my best interests.

Unless specifically limited, below, my Representative is authorized as follows:

A. To consent, refuse, or withdraw consent to any and all types of health care. Health care means any care, treatment, service or procedure to maintain, diagnose or otherwise affect an individual's physical or mental condition. It includes, but is not limited to, artificial respiration, nutritional support and hydration, medication and cardiopulmonary resuscitation;

B. To have access to medical records and information to the same extent that I am entitled, including the right to disclose the contents to others as appropriate for my health care;

C. To authorize my admission to or discharge (even against medical advice) from any hospital, nursing home, residential care, assisted living or similar facility or service;

D. To contract on my behalf for any health care related service or facility on my behalf, without my Representative incurring personal financial liability for such contracts;

E. To hire and fire medical, social service, and other support personnel responsible for my care;

F. To authorize, or refuse to authorize, any medication or procedure intended to relieve pain, even though such use may lead to physical damage, addiction, or hasten the moment of (but not intentionally cause) my death;

G. To make anatomical gifts of part or all of my body for medical purposes, authorize an autopsy, and direct the disposition of my remains, to the extent permitted by law;

H. To take any other action necessary to do what I authorize here, including (but not limited to) granting any waiver or release from liability required by any hospital, physician, or other health care provider; signing any documents relating to refusals of treatment or the leaving of a facility against medical advice; and pursuing any legal action in my name at the expense of my estate to force compliance with my wishes as determined by my Representative, or to seek actual or punitive damages for the failure to comply.

MY INSTRUCTIONS ABOUT END-OF-LIFE TREATMENT
(Initial only ONE of the following statements)

_____ NO SPECIFIC INSTRUCTIONS. My Representative knows my values and wishes, so I do not wish to include any specific instructions here.

DIRECTIVE TO WITHOLD OR WITHDRAW TREATMENT. Although I greatly value life, I also believe that at some point, life has such diminished value that medical treatment should be stopped, and I should be allowed to die. Therefore, I do not want to receive treatment, including nutrition and hydration, when the treatment will not give me a meaningful quality of life. I do not want my life prolonged . . .

_____ . . . if the treatment will leave me in a condition of permanent unconsciousness, such as with an irreversible coma or a persistent vegetative state.

_____ . . . if the treatment will leave me with no more than some consciousness and in an irreversible condition of complete, or nearly complete, loss of ability to think or communicate with others.

_____ . . . if the treatment will leave me with no more than some ability to think or communicate with others, and the likely risks and burdens of treatment outweigh the expected benefits. Risks, burdens and benefits include consideration of length of life, quality of life, financial costs, and my personal dignity and privacy.

_____ . . . DIRECTIVE TO RECEIVE TREATMENT. I want my life to be prolonged as long as possible, no matter what my quality of life.

_____ . . . DIRECTIVE ABOUT END-OF-LIFE TREATMENT IN MY OWN WORDS: _____

_____

_____

OTHER HEALTH CARE INSTRUCTIONS OF LIMITATIONS OR MODIFICATIONS OF MY REPRESENTATIVE'S POWERS
Be very careful about stating limitations, because the specific circumstances surrounding future health care decisions are impossible to predict. If you do not want any limitations, simply write "No Limitations." _____

_____

PROTECTION OF THIRD PARTIES WHO RELY ON MY REPRESENTATIVE
No person who relies in good faith upon any representations by my Representative or Alternate Representative(s) shall be liable to me, my estate, my heirs or assigns, for recognizing the Representative's authority.
Upon my death: (Initial one)

_____ I do not wish to donate any organs or tissue, OR

_____ I give any needed organs, tissues, or parts, OR

_____ I give only the following organs, tissues, or parts: (please

specify) _____

My gift (if any) is for the following purposes: (Initial your choices)

_____ Transplant

_____ Research

_____ Therapy

_____ Education

NOMINATION OF GUARDIAN
If a guardian of my person should for any reason need to be appointed, I nominate my Representative (or his or her alternate then authorized to act).

ADMINISTRATIVE PROVISIONS
▶ I revoke any prior health care advance directive.
▶ This health care advance directive is intended to be valid in any jurisdiction in which it is presented.
▶ A copy of this advance directive is intended to have the same effect as the original.

BY SIGNING HERE I INDICATE THAT I UNDERSTAND THE CONTENTS OF THIS DOCUMENT AND THE EFFECT OF THIS GRANT OF POWERS TO MY REPRESENTATIVE.

I sign my name to this Health Care Advance Directive on this _____ day of _____, in the year of_____.

My signature _____

My printed name _____

Current address _____

Witness signature _____ Date _____

Printed name _____

Current address _____

LIVING WILL DECLARATION

IN ST 16-36-4-10
IC 16-36-4-10

Declaration made this _____ day of _____, in the year
of _____. I, _____, being at least
eighteen (18) years of age and of sound mind, willfully and voluntarily make known my desires that my dying shall not be artificially
prolonged under the circumstances set forth below, and I declare:

If at any time my attending physician certifies in writing that: (1) I
have an incurable injury, disease, or illness; (2) my death will occur
within a short time; and (3) the use of life prolonging procedures
would serve only to artificially prolong the dying process, I direct
that such procedures be withheld or withdrawn, and that I be permitted to die naturally with only the performance or provision of
any medical procedure or medication necessary to provide me with
comfort care or to alleviate pain, and, if I have so indicated below,
the provision of artificially supplied nutrition and hydration. (Indicate your choice by initialing or making your mark before signing
this declaration)

_____ I wish to receive artificially supplied nutrition and hydration, even if the effort to sustain life is futile or excessively burden-
some to me.

_____ I do not wish to receive artificially supplied nutrition and
hydration, if the effort to sustain life is futile or excessively burden-
some to me.

_____ I intentionally make no decision concerning artificially supplied nutrition and hydration, leaving the decision to my health care
Representative appointed under IC 16-36-1-7 or my attorney in fact
with health care powers under IC-30-5-5.

In the absence of my ability to give directions regarding the use of
life prolonging procedures, it is my intention that this declaration

be honored by my family and physicians as the final expression of my legal right to refuse medical or surgical treatment and accept the consequences of the refusal.

I understand the full import of this declaration.

Signed _____

_____
(City, County, and State of Residence)

The declarant has been personally known to me, and I believe (him/her) to be of sound mind. I did not sign the declarant's signature above for or at the direction of the declarant. I am not a parent, spouse, or child of the declarant. I am not entitled to any part of the decarant's estate or directly financially responsible for the declarant's medical care. I am competent and at least eighteen (18) years of age.

Witness _____ Date _____

Witness _____ Date _____